# The History of Dragons

CRAFTED BY SKRIUWER

Copyright © 2024 by Skriuwer.

All rights reserved. No part of this book may be used or reproduced in any form whatsoever without written permission except in the case of brief quotations in critical articles or reviews.

At **Skriuwer**, we're more than just a team—we're a global community of people who love books. In Frisian, "Skriuwer" means "writer," and that's at the heart of what we do: creating and sharing books with readers worldwide. Wherever you are in the world, **Skriuwer** is here to inspire learning.

**Frisian** is one of the oldest languages in Europe, closely related to English and Dutch, and is spoken by about **500,000 people** in the province of **Friesland** (Fryslân), located in the northern Netherlands. It's the second official language of the Netherlands, but like many minority languages, Frisian faces the challenge of survival in a modern, globalized world.

We're using the money we earn to promote the Frisian language.

For more information, contact : **kontakt@skriuwer.com** (www.skriuwer.com)

# TABLE OF CONTENTS

## CHAPTER 1: EARLIEST GLIMPSES OF DRAGON MYTHS

- *Origins of serpent worship in prehistoric times*
- *Oral traditions forming the first proto-dragon ideas*
- *Environmental factors shaping early dragon concepts*

## CHAPTER 2: DRAGONS IN THE ANCIENT CIVILIZATIONS

- *Mesopotamian myths and the goddess Tiamat*
- *Egyptian serpent symbolism and Apophis*
- *Indus Valley and early serpent cults*

## CHAPTER 3: DRAGONS OF GREEK & ROMAN MYTHS

- *"Drakon" as giant serpent in Greek lore*
- *Famous dragon-slaying heroes (Hydra, Ladon, Python)*
- *Roman adaptations and the Mušḫuššu influence*

## CHAPTER 4: DRAGONS IN NORTHERN EUROPEAN LORE

- *Germanic wyrms and Celtic serpentine legends*
- *Fafnir, Nidhogg, and the Norse tradition*
- *Influence on Anglo-Saxon epics and folklore*

## CHAPTER 5: THE DRAGONS OF THE FAR EAST

- *Chinese imperial dragons and cosmic harmony*
- *Korean imugi and the path to dragonhood*
- *Japanese myths: Yamata no Orochi and water deities*

## CHAPTER 6: DRAGONS IN THE MIDDLE EAST & NORTH AFRICA

- *Persian Azhi Dahāka and Zoroastrian beliefs*
- *Biblical Leviathan and post-biblical traditions*
- *Local legends of monstrous serpents in desert regions*

## CHAPTER 7: DRAGONS ACROSS SUB-SAHARAN AFRICA

- *Water spirits and sacred pythons in West African lore*
- *Lake monsters and serpentine guardians in Central Africa*
- *Shifting roles in East and Southern African myth*

## CHAPTER 8: DRAGONS OF THE AMERICAS

- *Feathered serpent deities (Quetzalcoatl, Kukulkan)*
- *Andean Amaru and horned serpents of North America*
- *Symbolic roles of dragons in Mesoamerican and Andean cosmologies*

## CHAPTER 9: MEDIEVAL EUROPEAN DRAGONS & LEGENDS

- *Knights, saints, and the classic dragon-slaying motif*
- *Influence of bestiaries and church teaching*
- *Local folk tales blending heroic lore and communal identity*

## CHAPTER 10: DRAGONS IN EARLY CHRISTIAN WRITINGS

- *Book of Revelation and the red dragon*
- *Church Fathers' allegorical interpretations*
- *Saintly miracles and the dragon as demonic presence*

## CHAPTER 11: DRAGON ENCOUNTERS IN THE AGE OF EXPLORATION

- *Travelers' and missionaries' reports of monstrous reptiles*
- *Colonial curiosity and mapmakers' "Here be dragons"*
- *Rising skepticism alongside sensational travelogues*

## CHAPTER 12: DRAGON SYMBOLISM IN HERALDRY AND ART

- *Heraldic dragons, wyverns, and coats of arms*
- *Architectural gargoyles and decorative motifs*
- *Courtly pageants and grand visual representations*

## CHAPTER 13: DRAGONS IN THE RENAISSANCE WORLD

- *Humanist reexamination of classical serpents*
- *Renaissance art: blending realism with mythical themes*
- *Emerging scientific doubt but persistent popular fascination*

## CHAPTER 14: DRAGONS DURING THE EARLY ENLIGHTENMENT

- Empiricism and the rational dismissal of literal dragons
- Missionary narratives vs. scientific societies
- Shifting toward allegory and global cultural exchange

## CHAPTER 15: DRAGONS IN THE COLONIAL ERA

- Missionary conflicts and "dragon worship" abroad
- Colonial scientific surveys debunking sightings
- Syncretic myths and local resistance through serpent lore

## CHAPTER 16: DRAGONS IN NINETEENTH-CENTURY FOLKLORE

- Romantic nationalism and the rediscovery of dragon tales
- Folklorists collecting rural legends and epics
- Evolving moral lessons in children's fairy stories

## CHAPTER 17: DRAGONS IN EUROPEAN ROMANTIC MOVEMENTS

- Medieval revival and the dragon as symbol of the sublime
- Romantic poetry, art, and operatic grandeur
- Regional nuances in German, British, French, and Slavic contexts

## CHAPTER 18: DRAGON RELICS, SIGHTINGS, & STRANGE EVIDENCE

- Church displays of alleged "dragon bones"
- Colonial hoaxes and traveling curiosity shows
- Scientific dissections refuting relics and sightings

## CHAPTER 19: GROWING SKEPTICISM AND CHANGING VIEWS

- Late 19th-century shifts in belief and secularization
- Folklore's role in preserving symbolic dragons
- Reframing local relics and sightings as cultural heritage

## CHAPTER 20: THE LASTING LEGACY OF DRAGONS IN HISTORY

- Major historical roles and universal motifs
- Dragons' survival as national symbols and folklore treasures
- Reflections on the enduring human fascination with mythical beasts

# CHAPTER ONE: EARLIEST GLIMPSES OF DRAGON MYTHS

## Introduction

Dragons are among the most enduring mythical creatures in human history. Long before people had advanced systems of writing or complex civilizations, they told stories about reptilian monsters lurking in mysterious places. Sometimes these monsters were enormous serpents; sometimes they had limbs and wings. In the oldest archaeological traces we have, from simple carvings on rocks to crude paintings in caves, we see hints of the creatures that might have inspired dragon tales. It is hard to say if these earliest images truly represent "dragons," as we define them today, or if they show ordinary snakes, lizards, or crocodiles. However, many scholars believe that seeds of the dragon myth can be found in these ancient pieces of art.

The earliest glimpses of dragons are not just about images or carvings, though. They also come from the oral traditions that predate written history. Ancient people often passed down their stories, myths, and religious beliefs through word of mouth. Within these tales of gods, monsters, heroes, and natural wonders, we occasionally hear mention of giant serpents or powerful reptilian beings. Over time, with the start of writing systems in places like Sumer (in Mesopotamia) or the Indus Valley, these oral tales gained a more stable form.

In this first chapter, we will explore how the dragon concept may have taken shape in very early societies. We will look at the connection between large serpents and the fear or respect they inspired among ancient peoples. We will examine the ways that environmental factors, like the presence of real reptiles, might have contributed to the idea of dragons. We will also discuss how early beliefs about the cosmos and spiritual beings could have merged with simple observations of nature to form the first dragon myths.

Because we are dealing with preliterate history, the evidence is sparse. We rely on archaeology, comparative mythology, and educated guesses. While we cannot identify a single moment when someone said, "Here is a dragon," we can trace the rough outlines of how dragons may have emerged in the human mind. These outlines involve fear of the unknown, reverence for mighty creatures, and the need to explain strange happenings in the natural world.

## 1. The Roots of Serpent Worship and Fear

Even before the word "dragon" existed, large serpents held a significant place in many early societies. Snakes can inspire both fear and fascination. They are silent hunters, often venomous, and capable of killing animals much larger than themselves. Early human communities that encountered dangerous snakes regularly would develop stories and rituals to cope with the threat. Over time, these stories could grow into something bigger. In some cases, these stories turned serpents into divine or semi-divine figures.

Archaeological excavations in Africa, Asia, and parts of Europe have uncovered objects or cave paintings that might represent snakes. Though interpretations vary, some researchers see these as evidence of snake-related cults or worship. In many early societies, snakes were seen as symbols of rebirth because they shed their skin, revealing a fresh, shiny layer beneath. This ability sometimes made them symbols of immortality or cyclical time.

As human imagination developed, it is possible that people combined the qualities of snakes with other powerful animals, turning them into creatures that were more intimidating or symbolic. Think of a snake that grows larger in every retelling of a tale, eventually sprouting extra features such as horns, legs, or even wings. In many parts of the world, the word for "dragon" in ancient languages originally meant something closer to "serpent" or "giant snake."

For example, the Greek word "drakon," from which we get the modern word "dragon," can mean "serpent." Similar words appear in various ancient Indo-European languages. This suggests that long before the idea of the fully formed dragon with scales, wings, and fiery breath became widespread, people already had a sense that giant serpents could be more than just animals.

In these earliest glimpses, we can see how fear of a natural predator could blend with religious ideas, leading to the concept of a monstrous or sacred serpent. It might have been an invisible force that caused sickness or misfortune or a guardian of hidden knowledge. Over generations, these ideas could evolve further.

## 2. The Earliest Physical Depictions: Cave Art and Petroglyphs

One of the difficulties in tracing dragon myths back to prehistoric times is that we often do not know exactly what ancient artists intended to depict. A painted snake-like figure on a cave wall might represent a real snake. Or, it might represent a spirit or mythical being with reptilian features. Interpreting such art is tricky and depends on context, location, and comparisons with similar images.

Still, some caves have paintings of serpents with unusual shapes or patterns. In certain regions, these paintings are found near drawings of human figures in positions that might suggest a ritual. If we speculate that early humans created ceremonial areas in caves for religious or spiritual practices, it is possible that these serpent images held symbolic meaning. They could represent spirit guides, protective entities, or fearsome beasts that needed to be appeased.

Outside of caves, we also have stone carvings known as petroglyphs. These carvings often depict animals, hunts, and other scenes of daily life. In some, serpentine forms can be seen with horns or with abstract shapes above their heads. Without written records, it is impossible to say if these carvings portray an early dragon or a stylized version of a local snake. Yet, such images point to a longstanding tradition of giving serpents an important place in art and storytelling.

Many early agricultural societies also associated serpents with fertility and the land. As humans began to domesticate plants and animals, they watched how snakes emerged from holes in the ground or slithered through fields. A creature that could move between the surface world and underground realms might seem like a messenger between humans and the spirits of the earth. From there, it is not hard to imagine that some storytellers added further mystical qualities.

## 3. Oral Traditions: The Birth of Legendary Serpents

Before the widespread use of writing, stories were told and retold. Each time, a tale might grow. A snake with unusual coloration could become a mammoth serpent in the next telling, and eventually, it could be described as an impossible creature of great power. In tight-knit communities, these stories would be shared around fires, repeated during communal gatherings, and passed from generation to generation.

In many prehistoric cultures, the people believed that the world was full of spirits. Dangerous animals, like bears or big cats, were seen as embodiments of certain forces. Snakes, however, held a unique place because of their venom. Many groups believed that venom was a kind of magical poison. They told stories that snakes might hold the secret to life or death. Over time, this notion could blend with other spiritual ideas, leading to the idea that certain snakes were not normal animals but guardians of some hidden realm or knowledge.

Sometimes, these mythical serpents guarded precious resources—like water sources in arid regions—or special items—like sacred stones or metals. These tales might have started from real-life encounters. A snake living near a water hole could become a local terror. Then, people began saying that the snake was larger than normal, that it had special powers, that it could appear or disappear at will. Thus, a legend took shape. Eventually, the serpent might sprout horns in the stories, or it might become more dragon-like with each retelling.

These early oral myths acted as the seed for what later civilizations would write down as dragon stories. Each region had its own flavor, influenced by the local wildlife, climate, and cultural beliefs. In some areas, dragons would be water creatures; in others, they would dwell in mountains or deserts. But the core idea of a serpentine being with powers beyond a normal animal was fairly common.

## 4. Environmental Factors and the Rise of the "Dragon" Concept

The environment played a huge role in shaping people's perceptions of mythical creatures. For instance, places prone to floods might have stories of serpents that controlled the water. In regions with tall mountain ranges, legends might speak of serpents or beasts lurking in high caves, able to breathe out cold winds or mists. Where volcanoes were active, some communities might imagine fiery serpents beneath the earth, controlling lava flows or causing eruptions.

Moreover, fossils discovered by ancient peoples could have contributed to the idea of dragons. Large dinosaur bones might have been found by chance. Without knowledge of paleontology, early humans could only guess what sort of creature these bones belonged to. They might have concluded that giant, fearsome beasts once walked the earth. This might explain why certain dragon myths speak of creatures that once were common but later vanished or retreated to hidden realms. Although we do not have direct prehistoric testimonies of fossil discoveries leading to dragon legends, some scholars suspect a link.

Climatic changes over thousands of years could also influence myths. A tribe living in a region that slowly became drier might say that a serpent spirit stole the rain. Another group that suffered from coastal storms might blame a monstrous sea serpent for churning up the waves. In each case, the forces of nature became personified as reptiles or serpentine beings. Over centuries, these stories could expand, linking to the concept of a dragon who governed weather, water, and the earth.

## 5. Early Rituals and the Emergence of Serpentine Gods

As societies grew more complex, so did their rituals. Shamans or spiritual leaders conducted ceremonies to control or appease the forces they feared. In some cultures, these ceremonies might have included offerings to serpentine gods or spirits. Eventually, certain communities could develop an entire religious system that placed a serpent-like deity at its center.

These gods might have required sacrifices—crops, animals, or even, in certain extreme legends, human offerings. People believed that if they satisfied these serpent deities, they would get rain for their fields, protection from disease, or victory in tribal conflicts. Over time, the serpent deities often took on more elaborate forms. Statues or carvings might have shown them with the heads of snakes and bodies of humans, or full reptilian bodies with added features like wings or horns.

The line between a revered serpent god and what we might call a "dragon" starts to blur in these ancient religious contexts. While we typically associate dragons with later civilizations like the Chinese or the Europeans, the basic idea that a reptilian being could hold supernatural power is present from these earliest periods. Because each community shaped its gods in its own way, we see many different expressions of serpent worship. Some remain purely snake-like, but others grow more monstrous in artistic depictions.

## 6. Distinguishing Between Giant Serpents and Proto-Dragons

It is not always easy to say when a giant serpent in a story officially becomes a "dragon." Our modern image of a dragon often includes wings, legs, fiery breath, or a spiked tail. But the earliest glimpses of dragons were likely much simpler. Many myths do not mention wings at all. Instead, they speak of a serpent so large it circles the earth or blocks out the sun.

Some scholars propose that the dragon concept might have originated in different places independently. One region might have started with a large serpent that gradually gained other features in myths. Another region might have merged the lion, eagle, and serpent to form a chimeric beast. As humans interacted through trade, migration, and conquest, these ideas could spread, merge, and evolve into the recognizable dragons we see in the art of later civilizations.

Another factor that contributed to the difference between giant serpents and proto-dragons was the role of storytelling in shaping cultural identity. A tribe might talk about a monstrous serpent to assert their own bravery or claim that their ancestors overcame it. Over time, telling of that victory might grow grander, and the serpent might turn into a multi-headed beast. Later, it might gain a name, a distinct personality, and a place in the community's religious or cultural rituals. In this sense, the "dragon" was born not from a single event but from an ongoing process of storytelling.

## 7. Early Evidence from Excavations and Artifacts

While most prehistoric cultures did not leave written records, some left behind artifacts that hint at their beliefs. In addition to cave paintings and petroglyphs, archaeologists have found small sculptures or amulets shaped like snakes or snake-headed figures. Some of these date back thousands of years, indicating that serpent-related symbolism was important.

One of the challenges is determining whether an artifact depicts a mere serpent or something more mythical. Some sculptures show reptilian creatures with human-like faces, or with decorative patterns that suggest a ceremonial function. In certain finds, the creature appears to have multiple heads, or it is shown devouring a smaller figure that might represent a human. These could be early representations of monstrous serpents that we might label as "proto-dragons."

Occasionally, burial sites include offerings shaped like snakes or carved from bones that could have come from large reptiles. If these remains were treated with special care, it might suggest a belief in the serpent's power over death or the afterlife. There is also evidence that some grave goods featured stylized reptilian motifs, possibly as protective symbols for the dead. All of these findings, while not conclusive proof of early dragon worship, reveal that serpents were deeply woven into the spiritual fabric of prehistoric societies.

## 8. Transition to Written Records and Emerging Dragon Lore

As writing emerged in places like Mesopotamia, Egypt, and the Indus Valley, many older oral traditions began to appear in written form. These earliest written stories include creation myths, epic poems, and religious texts. Among these, we sometimes find references to serpent-like monsters or chaos creatures that threaten gods or humans.

For instance, in some Mesopotamian myths, the goddess Tiamat is described as a serpent or a dragon figure representing the primeval sea. While Tiamat belongs more properly to the realm of recorded ancient history, her story might echo older traditions that existed among preliterate groups in that region. In this sense, the line between "prehistory" and "history" is blurred.

Nevertheless, the earliest glimpses of dragon myths belong to that time before extensive written documentation, when fear, awe, and respect for serpentine powers formed a basic part of many societies. By the time writing came into wide use, the idea of serpent-like monsters was already deeply established. We see them appear as cosmic foes, guardians of treasures, or symbols of royalty and divinity.

Thus, the stage was set for the many different dragon traditions that would follow. The earliest glimpses reveal how ancient peoples, lacking modern explanations for the natural world, wove tales of giant serpents and reptilian beings to explain both everyday dangers and cosmic mysteries. These proto-dragon figures would become the foundation for the more developed dragon myths we find in ancient and classical civilizations.

# CHAPTER TWO: DRAGONS IN THE ANCIENT CIVILIZATIONS

## Introduction

By the time civilizations rose in Mesopotamia, Egypt, the Indus Valley, and beyond, the idea of monstrous serpents or dragon-like beings was well-established. Now we begin to see these creatures recorded in writing, depicted in more refined art, and placed in religious texts or epic narratives. The stories are no longer vague references passed down orally. Instead, they take on structured forms that detail the roles these creatures played in society.

In this chapter, we will look at how various ancient civilizations portrayed dragons or dragon-like creatures. We will explore some of the earliest written myths, such as those from Sumer, Babylon, and Assyria, as well as the beginnings of dragon lore in ancient Egypt and the Indus Valley. Each civilization had its own unique style and interpretation of these creatures, influenced by geography, religious beliefs, and social structures.

We will also see how dragons appeared as symbols of power and protection. Rulers might adopt dragon imagery to show their strength, while temples might feature dragon motifs to signify a link to the gods. In some cases, dragons were seen as chaotic forces that needed to be defeated by heroic gods. In others, they were protectors of sacred objects or even the embodiment of a deity itself.

## 1. Sumerian and Babylonian Dragons

The region of Mesopotamia, often called the cradle of civilization, saw the rise of Sumerian city-states such as Uruk, Ur, and Eridu. These cities flourished around the fourth millennium BCE, leaving behind some of the oldest written texts on clay tablets. Among these texts are myths, hymns, and epic stories that feature references to monstrous serpents or creatures that we might consider dragon-like.

One of the earliest known stories is the "Enki and the World Order," which touches on the distribution of powers among gods. While not a dragon narrative per se, this text hints at a belief in supernatural creatures dwelling in the waters. More directly related to dragons is the character of Kur, an entity sometimes interpreted as a giant serpent. In some writings, Kur is described as living in the netherworld or watery depths, controlling certain domains that pose danger to humans and gods alike.

As we move into the Babylonian period, myths become more elaborate. The Epic of Creation, also known as the "Enuma Elish," introduces Tiamat, a primordial goddess of saltwater. She is often described as a terrible serpent or dragon. Although the cuneiform texts vary in details, it is generally agreed that Tiamat takes on the form of a giant monster to battle the younger gods. Marduk, a chief deity, eventually slays Tiamat, using her body to form parts of the cosmos.

Tiamat's depiction is key to understanding how ancient Mesopotamians viewed dragons. She represents chaos, the formless waters, and an untamed primal force. By defeating her, Marduk brings order to the universe. This concept of a serpentine or dragon-like being as chaos incarnate would influence later myths in other cultures as well.

Babylonians also depicted dragons in art. The famous Ishtar Gate, constructed by King Nebuchadnezzar II around the 6th century BCE, shows images of mušḫuššu (sometimes called the "Sirrush"). This creature is a dragon-like figure with a serpent's body, lion-like forelimbs, and bird-like hind legs. It appears alongside other sacred animals on the glazed bricks of the gate. The mušḫuššu served as a symbol of the city's chief god, Marduk, reinforcing the connection between dragon imagery and divine power in Babylonian culture.

## 2. Assyrian Interpretations and Continuations

The Assyrians, who emerged as a dominant power in northern Mesopotamia, inherited many aspects of Sumerian and Babylonian religion. Their myths also mention serpentine monsters and chaos creatures, often linked to floods or destructive events. In Assyrian art, we see stylized dragons and serpentine beings on palace reliefs, indicating that the concept of a dragon or monstrous serpent was widespread throughout Mesopotamia.

In some Assyrian texts, references to sea serpents or chaos dragons are made in hymns or ritual incantations. These texts might invoke the gods to protect the kingdom from the dangers represented by these creatures. Although details can differ from one city to another, the underlying theme remains: serpentine or dragon-like monsters stand for threats that must be overcome by the divine or by the king acting under divine authority.

In this context, dragons were not simply random beasts. They symbolized the deeper fears and hopes of a society that faced floods, droughts, wars, and other hardships. A victorious god or king who could conquer a dragon was thus seen as a bringer of order, fertility, and safety.

## 3. Early Dragon Lore in Ancient Egypt

Egyptian culture developed along the fertile banks of the Nile. While we often associate Egypt with gods that have human bodies and animal heads, serpents also played a vital role in Egyptian mythology. One prominent figure is Apophis (Apep), often described as a giant serpent or serpent-demon that threatened the sun god Ra.

In Egyptian cosmology, Apophis personifies chaos, lying in wait each night to attack Ra's solar barge as it travels through the underworld. If Apophis succeeded, darkness and disorder would triumph. However, Ra and his helpers subdue Apophis every night, ensuring the sun rises again. This cyclical battle can be viewed as a cosmic fight between order (Ma'at) and chaos (Isfet).

Apophis is sometimes illustrated as a huge snake with ominous features, though Egyptian art rarely shows the typical dragon shape we might imagine. Still, the concept of a chaos serpent that must be vanquished is similar to the Mesopotamian theme of gods defeating chaotic serpent monsters (like Marduk defeating Tiamat). This shows a broader pattern in ancient Near Eastern beliefs: a cosmic serpent stands for primordial disorder, and each morning or new year is a symbolic victory over that chaos.

Beyond Apophis, Egypt had other serpent-like deities and symbols. The uraeus, a rearing cobra worn on the crowns of pharaohs, symbolized protection and divine authority. While not a full dragon, the cobra itself had a powerful significance, able to spit venom and strike from the shadows. Over time, the idea of a protective serpent around a ruler might mix with more monstrous or mythical interpretations, though in Egyptian art, we see more stylized snakes than winged dragons.

In funerary texts, serpents and serpent guardians appear often. They can either threaten the deceased or protect sacred passages. The idea of reptilian entities with supernatural abilities was not alien to the Egyptians. Although we do not find many direct references to "dragons" in Egyptian texts, the repeated presence of serpentine foes and protectors alike sets a foundation that could be linked to a broader dragon tradition in the ancient world.

## 4. The Indus Valley and Early Hindu Myths

While the Indus Valley Civilization (circa 3300–1300 BCE) did not leave clear references to dragons as we know them, we do find evidence of snake worship. Seals and artifacts from sites like Mohenjo-daro and Harappa sometimes show creatures that are part human, part serpent. These could be early forms of the Naga concept that appears in later Hindu, Buddhist, and Jain traditions.

Nagas, in the Indian subcontinent's later mythology, are serpent beings that can shape-shift and often dwell in underwater realms. While not always described as dragons, the Naga concept includes features like multiple heads and a powerful connection to water. In some stories, Nagas guard treasures or hidden knowledge. In others, they can be hostile and cause floods or other disasters.

These earlier Indus artifacts do not explicitly mention the name "Naga." However, the repeated serpent imagery points to a cultural fascination with snake-like beings. As Vedic culture developed and merged with local traditions, it is plausible that existing serpent myths evolved into the elaborate forms we see in Hindu texts.

Though we lack direct Indus Valley texts describing a monstrous serpent or dragon, the strong presence of serpent worship in South Asia suggests that the region had its own share of giant snake legends. Later writings, such as the Mahabharata and Puranas, would feature many accounts of powerful serpentine beings, some of whom rival the "dragon" concept in scale and might.

## 5. Anatolia, the Levant, and the Serpent-Dragon Archetype

Moving west and north from Mesopotamia, we encounter ancient Anatolia (modern-day Turkey) and the Levant (the eastern Mediterranean region). Hittite, Hurrian, and Canaanite myths also speak of serpent or dragon-like creatures. The Hittite "Illuyanka" myth, for example, describes a serpent (Illuyanka) that battles the weather god. Though the creature is not always depicted as a winged beast, it is described as a dangerous reptilian foe that must be tricked or overpowered.

In Canaanite lore, we find references to Lotan or Leviathan, a sea monster sometimes described as a many-headed serpent. Although these texts come from a slightly later period, they likely have roots in older traditions. The theme is consistent with the broader Near Eastern pattern: a storm or warrior god defeats a chaos serpent, ensuring the stability of the world.

Leviathan would later appear in Hebrew scriptures and other sources, sometimes framed as a primeval dragon or sea monster. This early tradition in the Levant set the stage for how dragons could be interpreted in biblical and related texts. Even though these developments belong to a period somewhat later than the earliest civilizations, the seeds of the serpent-dragon archetype can be found in these older myths.

## 6. Dragons as Symbols of Royalty and Divine Power

In many ancient cultures, monstrous serpents or dragons did not only represent chaos. Sometimes they symbolized royal or divine power. Rulers might adopt dragon imagery to show they had the favor of gods who had previously conquered serpentine forces. Alternatively, the rulers might claim descent from a dragon or serpent deity, implying they had the same fierce, magical qualities.

As noted with the Babylonian mušḫuššu or the Egyptian uraeus, the presence of a dragon-like emblem on palace walls or crowns was a statement of legitimacy. It said, "I have harnessed the power of chaos," or "I am protected by the might of the serpent." Over time, this association would grow stronger, influencing how later civilizations used dragon motifs in official seals, flags, or armor.

In ancient China—though this civilization developed somewhat separately—similar ideas took hold. (Chinese dragons are explored in more depth in a later chapter, but it is worth noting here that they, too, came to symbolize imperial authority and cosmic power.) This broader trend across many civilizations suggests that the dragon, in one form or another, was a versatile symbol: it could represent both chaos that must be defeated and the ultimate power that legitimizes a ruler.

## 7. Religious Ceremonies and Myths of Cosmic Struggle

Across these ancient civilizations, the struggle between order and chaos was a recurring theme. Dragon-like creatures often found themselves on the side of chaos, resisting the efforts of the gods to bring harmony. This cosmic drama was not just a story but a reflection of how ancient societies understood their world. The annual floods of the Nile, the Tigris, and the Euphrates could be both life-giving and destructive. The unpredictability of weather, earthquakes, and disease suggested that chaos was always lurking.

In religious ceremonies, priests and worshippers might reenact the defeat of a serpent or chaos monster to ensure the continuation of cosmic balance. For example, Egyptian priests performed rituals to help Ra overcome Apophis. Babylonians likely had ceremonies praising Marduk's victory over Tiamat. These rituals gave people a sense of control over natural and supernatural forces.

In that sense, dragons or giant serpents became more than just stories; they were woven into the fabric of temple rites, kingship ceremonies, and seasonal festivals. The creatures represented a tangible focus for fears about destructive forces. By venerating the gods who conquered these creatures, or by honoring the serpents themselves if they were protective or divine, communities believed they could secure prosperity and safety.

## 8. Cultural Exchanges and the Spread of Dragon Lore

Trade routes crisscrossed the ancient world, connecting Mesopotamia, the Indus Valley, Egypt, Anatolia, and beyond. Merchants, soldiers, and migrants carried not only goods but also stories and beliefs. As a result, ideas about serpents and dragon-like monsters could travel from one region to another.

This exchange is evident in how certain motifs recur in different civilizations. The basic image of a heroic storm or sky god defeating a giant reptilian monster appears in various myths across the Near East. Some scholars suggest that these stories might share an even older common source, or that one myth directly influenced another as cultures interacted.

Over time, details changed. Some dragons gained multiple heads; some developed wings; others stayed in watery habitats or deserts. Nonetheless, the underlying concept of a powerful serpentine creature remained. This shared narrative contributed to a sense of familiarity, even when people from different cultures met. They might use different names—Tiamat, Apophis, Leviathan, Illuyanka—but they often recognized the same fundamental struggle between order and chaos.

## 9. Shaping Later Myths and Legends

The dragon stories found in ancient civilizations laid the groundwork for many later mythologies. Greek and Roman tales of serpentine monsters, which will be covered in the next chapters, owe a debt to the earlier traditions in the Near East and Egypt. Even the dragons of medieval Europe, centuries later, can be traced to some of these old narrative patterns—particularly the theme of a hero defeating a dragon, thereby establishing order or proving worthiness.

In the East, similar developments took place. Though Chinese dragons evolved somewhat independently, they still carried the dual symbolism of power and mystery, often controlling weather and water. Some scholars point to possible links between Western and Eastern dragon lore through the trade networks of the Silk Road, although direct evidence is sparse.

For the ancient Egyptians, Mesopotamians, and others, the line between religion, myth, and daily life was thin. Their gods walked among them in stories, and monstrous serpents lurked in the boundaries of the known world. Whether revered as protective beings or feared as agents of chaos, dragons and dragon-like creatures formed a key part of how these civilizations explained the forces around them.

# CHAPTER THREE: DRAGONS OF GREEK AND ROMAN MYTHS

## Introduction

Greek and Roman stories have shaped much of Western understanding of mythology, including how people picture dragons or dragon-like creatures. These ancient civilizations inherited older ideas from places like Mesopotamia and Egypt, but they also developed their own original myths and symbols. The Greek and Roman worlds produced well-known tales of serpentine monsters—some winged, some multi-headed, and others more like giant snakes. In many cases, these creatures guarded sacred places or precious treasures, requiring a hero or a god to defeat them.

Greek myths spoke of dragons in epics, poems, and plays. Some creatures, such as the Hydra or the Colchian Dragon, were connected to famous legends like the Labors of Heracles or the quest for the Golden Fleece. Others were bound to important religious sites, such as the serpent Python at Delphi. Over time, the Romans adapted many of these Greek tales, blending them with their own beliefs and giving them a Roman flavor.

This chapter will examine major Greek dragon myths, including the well-known examples of Python, Hydra, Ladon, Typhon, and other dragon-like beings called "drakons." We will also see how these myths shifted under Roman rule and how the concept of the dragon—sometimes referred to as *draco* in Latin—became tied to Roman symbolism. By looking at these stories in detail, we can see how dragons moved from being primal monsters to meaningful symbols in ancient literature and culture.

---

## 1. The Greek Term "Drakon" and Its Early Uses

In ancient Greek, the word "drakon" (δράκων) generally meant "serpent" or "giant serpent." It did not always refer to a winged monster breathing fire. Often, a "drakon" was a large snake or a snake-like creature imbued with supernatural power. Over time, the word "drakon" came to describe any formidable reptilian beast, whether or not it had extra features like multiple heads or wings.

Greek poets and playwrights used the term in different ways. In *Theogony*, Hesiod mentions serpents born from divine beings, mixing them into genealogies of monsters. In some passages, the term "drakon" might refer to a literal snake, while in others, it points to a monstrous being that surpasses any normal animal. The difference often lies in the context: if it is a fearful guardian of a sacred grove or a monstrous opponent for a hero, it is likely no ordinary snake.

Because of this linguistic flexibility, we see a wide variety of drakons in Greek myth. Some stay close to the image of a large viper or python. Others gain more extraordinary qualities, like breathing poisonous fumes or having the ability to speak. The stories often revolve around conflict, with a god or hero seeking to overcome the creature in order to claim a resource or prove worthiness. In a sense, these early Greek "dragons" lay the groundwork for the more elaborate dragons found in later Western culture, even if their original forms might differ from modern expectations.

## 2. Python: The Earth Dragon of Delphi

One of the earliest known dragon figures in Greek mythology is Python, sometimes called simply the Delphic serpent. According to various sources, Python was a monstrous serpent that lived near Delphi, an important religious site dedicated to the god Apollo. The myth says that the serpent guarded the area around the Castalian Spring or lived in a cave where the oracle of Delphi would later reside.

### Origin and Role
Python was described as an offspring of Gaia (the Earth) or, in some versions, created by the goddess Hera to trouble Leto, Apollo's mother. Its presence at Delphi indicated a powerful earth force. Snakes and serpents were often linked to chthonic (underworld or earth-related) powers, signifying deeper mysteries and ties to the earth's energy. Because Delphi was seen as a navel of the world (the omphalos), Python's existence there underscored the site's ancient, primal nature.

### The Battle with Apollo
In the most common version of the myth, Apollo sought to build his temple at

Delphi, but Python stood in his way. A young god, Apollo hunted and killed Python with his bow. By slaying the serpent, Apollo claimed Delphi as his own sacred place. Afterward, the oracle there would give prophecies under Apollo's guidance, though some traditions say the oracle was originally linked to Gaia and that Apollo took over after defeating Python.

**Cultural Importance**
This myth symbolizes the shift from older, earth-based deities to the Olympian gods. The victory of Apollo suggests the triumph of a newer order over archaic powers. In religious practice, the Pythian Games were held at Delphi every four years, honoring Apollo's victory over the serpent. The name "Pythian" itself comes from Python. This shows how closely the legend was tied to local worship and cultural identity.

**Dragon-Like Qualities**
Although Python was called a serpent, many later depictions show it as more monstrous than a normal snake. Its size was said to be immense, and its presence was threatening enough to require Apollo's direct intervention. While not described with wings or fire, it fits the basic idea of a "drakon": a huge, deadly reptile linked to a sacred site and confronting a divine or heroic challenger.

---

## 3. The Lernaean Hydra

Probably the most famous Greek dragon-like creature is the Lernaean Hydra, encountered by the hero Heracles (Hercules in Roman tradition) during his Twelve Labors. The Hydra dwelled in the marshes of Lerna and had multiple heads—usually nine, but some versions say more. One head was immortal, and if Heracles cut off any of the other heads, two would grow back in its place.

**Origins of the Hydra**
The Hydra was often described as a child of Typhon and Echidna, themselves monstrous figures. Typhon, in particular, was the father of many beasts in Greek myth, linking the Hydra to a broader family of monsters. This lineage placed the Hydra firmly in the category of divine or semi-divine creatures rather than mere animals.

## The Second Labor of Heracles

As part of his penance, Heracles had to slay the Hydra. He discovered that simply cutting off the creature's heads was futile. With the help of his nephew Iolaus, he used fire to cauterize the stumps as soon as he chopped off each head, preventing them from regrowing. Finally, he buried the immortal head under a large rock. This combination of brute strength and cunning led to the Hydra's defeat.

## Symbolic Meaning

The Lernaean Hydra stood for a seemingly unstoppable threat. Each new head that grew back represented the ongoing challenges one faces in life or the idea that evil can proliferate if not fully conquered. By finding a strategic way to stop the regrowth, Heracles showed his heroic ingenuity and earned a place among the greatest mythic figures.

## A "Dragon" or a "Serpent"?

In art, the Hydra is often depicted with multiple serpent-like heads emerging from a single torso. Its body sometimes has reptilian legs or a long tail, making it look more like a dragon. Ancient texts use the term "drakon" or refer to it as a water serpent. Over time, especially in later retellings, the Hydra's image shifted to be even more dragon-like, emphasizing its monstrous nature.

---

# 4. The Colchian Dragon and the Golden Fleece

Another well-known serpentine guardian in Greek myth is the dragon that guarded the Golden Fleece in Colchis, a region at the far edge of the Greek world (often identified with the eastern coast of the Black Sea). This creature appears in the story of Jason and the Argonauts, as told in *Apollonius of Rhodes' Argonautica* and other later sources.

## The Dragon of Ares

The Colchian Dragon was sometimes said to be sacred to the war god Ares. Its role was to protect the Golden Fleece hanging in a grove of trees. Being devoted to a god of war, the dragon had a fierce reputation. Many versions describe it as colossal in size, coiled around the tree and ever-watchful, never sleeping.

## Medea's Magical Aid

When Jason arrived in Colchis to claim the Golden Fleece, the most formidable obstacle was the dragon. However, Medea, a sorceress and the daughter of King Aeëtes, assisted him. According to some stories, she used potions or magic spells to lull the dragon to sleep, allowing Jason to seize the fleece without fighting the creature directly. In other accounts, Jason manages to kill or wound the dragon, but the more common version emphasizes Medea's cunning and magical arts.

**A Symbol of Distant Danger**
The Colchian Dragon was set in a region viewed as exotic and far from mainland Greece. Its presence highlighted the perils of venturing into unknown lands. It also underscored the idea that great treasures are protected by fearsome creatures, a theme seen across various myths. Though the dragon itself does not have an extensive backstory, it serves as a key plot element, reinforcing the heroic challenge Jason must overcome.

**Shaping Later Perceptions**
Because the quest for the Golden Fleece is a foundational Greek epic, the image of the Colchian Dragon became a model for many "treasure-guarding dragons" in subsequent narratives. Later authors and artists depicted it with glowing eyes, shimmering scales, and immense coils. This helped solidify the trope of the dragon as a vigilant guardian of riches.

---

## 5. Ladon: The Dragon of the Hesperides

Ladon is another guardian dragon from Greek mythology. He guarded the golden apples of the Hesperides, precious fruits that conferred immortality or eternal youth. This dragon is described as having a coiled serpent body and, in some versions, a hundred heads. Like the Hydra, Ladon was often named as a child of Typhon and Echidna, reinforcing the theme of monstrous parentage.

**Setting and Role**
The Hesperides were nymphs who lived in a garden at the western edge of the world, near the Atlas Mountains. Their golden apples were gifts from Gaia to Hera, meant to represent divine blessing. Ladon's duty was to prevent anyone from taking these apples. Since the apples symbolized eternal youth and godly favor, guarding them was a high-stakes task.

**Encounter with Heracles**
One of Heracles' Twelve Labors involved obtaining these golden apples. Different

versions of the story provide different outcomes for Ladon. In some accounts, Heracles slays the dragon outright. In others, he uses trickery—persuading Atlas to fetch the apples—so Ladon is bypassed. Regardless, Ladon is a formidable opponent, part of the same monstrous family tree that includes other famous dragons in Greek lore.

**Artistic Depictions and Legacy**
Ancient vase paintings and later artworks sometimes show Ladon as a serpentine dragon coiled around a tree with apples. Over time, the story of Ladon guarding a tree with precious fruit became a widespread motif, influencing how dragons were seen in later European tales about guardians of orchards, groves, or magical items.

---

## 6. Typhon: The Father of Monsters

Typhon stands out as one of the most colossal and terrifying figures in Greek mythology. Often described with dozens of snake heads or with serpents writhing around his limbs, he was said to be the strongest offspring of Gaia or born from Tartarus. Sometimes, accounts depict him as a winged being covered in serpentine coils, with dragon-like features that surpass all others.

**Typhon's Battle with Zeus**
The most famous story involving Typhon is his cosmic battle against Zeus for supremacy over the cosmos. Typhon was so powerful that he managed to wound Zeus and strip him of his sinews in some versions. However, Hermes helped restore Zeus's strength, and the king of the gods eventually hurled thunderbolts at Typhon, trapping him beneath Mount Etna in Sicily.

**Connection to Dragon Lore**
While Typhon might be called a giant or a monstrous titan, his many serpent heads and fiery breath align him with dragon imagery. He is sometimes listed as the father (or mother in some unusual references) of various beasts, including Cerberus, the Hydra, and the Chimera. This lineage cements Typhon's place at the root of Greek monstrous mythology.

**Symbolic Interpretation**
Typhon represents an older, more chaotic force that threatens the established order of the Olympian gods. Much like Tiamat in Mesopotamian myths or

Apophis in Egyptian lore, Typhon is a figure of raw chaos. His defeat by Zeus supports the cosmic order that the Olympians bring. He also serves as the ultimate test of Zeus's power, showing that even the greatest chaos can be subdued by divine authority.

## 7. Drakaina: Female Dragons and Serpent Women

Greek myth also includes references to drakainas, or female dragons. These might appear as half-woman, half-serpent beings, or simply as monstrous serpents of feminine aspect. One notable example is Echidna, often called the "Mother of Monsters." She was sometimes depicted as a woman from the waist up and a snake from the waist down, dwelling in remote caves.

**Echidna's Offspring**
Echidna and Typhon produced many of the monstrous dragons and beasts of Greek myth, such as the Hydra, Cerberus, and the Chimera. Echidna herself did not always appear as a direct enemy for heroes, but she symbolized the wellspring of chaotic or monstrous life. Her presence in myths underscores the idea that monstrous creatures arise from a primordial, almost divine source.

**Other Examples**
Some local legends spoke of drakainas that tormented travelers or guarded springs. Heroes like Bellerophon or Perseus might face such creatures in lesser-known stories. Often, these female dragons possessed cunning or magical abilities, making them dangerous foes. While they are not always central to major myths, their presence highlights the diversity within Greek dragon lore: not all serpents or dragons were the same; some had strong female or maternal traits tied to the earth.

## 8. Dragons in Greek Epic, Poetry, and Drama

Dragons appear in many different literary genres in ancient Greece. Epics such as Hesiod's *Theogony* and Apollonius's *Argonautica* describe the genealogies and battles of monstrous serpents. Poems and plays might also mention dragons in passing, using them as symbols of ultimate danger or as powerful guardians.

- **Homer's Works**: In *The Iliad* and *The Odyssey*, the word "drakon" can appear, sometimes referring to an ordinary snake but also implying something more ominous. Though Homer does not feature a major dragon-focused narrative, the presence of serpents or monstrous guardians is hinted at in certain passages.
- **Tragedians**: Playwrights like Euripides and Sophocles mention dragon-like creatures in their works, especially when recounting heroic myths. They often treat the dragon as a test of valor or a symbol of divine retribution.
- **Local Legends**: City-states had their own tales of serpents or dragons. These local myths might celebrate a founder-hero who killed a dragon or might revolve around a sacred dragon linked to a city's well-being.

In each case, dragons served a dramatic function: they were the extreme threat that only the bravest or the favored by gods could overcome. This pattern of pitting a hero against a dragon would later become a staple in European literature for centuries.

---

## 9. Roman Adoption of Greek Dragon Myths

When Rome expanded and absorbed Greek territories, it also adopted Greek culture and mythology. Roman writers like Ovid, Virgil, and others retold Greek myths in Latin, preserving and reshaping many dragon tales for Roman audiences.

### Heracles Becomes Hercules
The Twelve Labors of Heracles became the Twelve Labors of Hercules. The Hydra, Ladon, and other serpentine foes remained part of these stories, now couched in Roman language and style. Roman art often depicted the heroic figure of Hercules in battle with the Hydra, making it a frequent motif on mosaics or relief sculptures.

### Argonauts and Other Heroes
Likewise, the tale of Jason and the Argonauts underwent Roman interpretation, with the Colchian Dragon continuing as a formidable guard of the Golden Fleece. Roman poets and playwrights sometimes added flourishes, but the basic concept of a heroic quest facing off against a dragon-like beast remained the same.

**Preservation and Adaptation**
By translating and reinterpreting Greek works, the Romans ensured these dragon myths endured. Even as the Roman Empire spread across Europe and parts of the Middle East, these tales of serpents and dragons accompanied them. Over time, local populations might merge their own dragon traditions with the Greek-Roman versions, leading to a broader tapestry of dragon lore.

## 10. The Draco Standard in the Roman Army

An interesting aspect of Roman culture was the use of the *draco* (dragon) as a military standard. Adopted from Eastern cavalry units—possibly from the Dacians or Sarmatians—the *draco* was a windsock-like device shaped like a dragon's head with a fabric body. When mounted on a lance and carried at high speed, the wind would rush through the dragon's open mouth, causing the cloth to stream behind, giving the impression of a serpentine creature in flight.

**Origin and Spread**
Although Greek myths had long featured serpents called drakons, the Roman *draco* standard seems to have come from contact with steppe peoples who had their own dragon symbolism. The Romans found it striking and integrated it into some of their cavalry units.

**Symbolic Meaning**
Carrying a dragon-headed standard could intimidate enemies and boost the morale of Roman troops. Over time, the *draco* became an emblem associated with certain legions, signifying bravery, speed, and fearlessness. This military usage of dragon imagery highlights how dragons moved beyond myth into practical, real-world symbolism for power and prestige in the ancient world.

**Influence on Later Traditions**
The Roman *draco* standard survived into the Byzantine period, and from there, it may have influenced medieval European heraldry. Though the user specifically asked to keep modern times out of the discussion, it is worth noting that the transformation of the dragon from a purely mythic creature to a recognized symbol of war had its roots in the Roman era.

## 11. Dragons in Roman Literature and Natural Philosophy

Roman authors sometimes wrote about exotic animals or monsters in works that combined myth, history, and observation. Writers like Pliny the Elder, in his *Natural History*, included mentions of dragons as real creatures living in distant lands, often in India or Ethiopia. These "dragons" might have been large snakes or pythons, but rumors and secondhand accounts inflated them into massive serpentine beasts capable of strangling elephants.

### Myth vs. Reality
Many Romans did not draw a strict line between real animals and legendary creatures. If travelers or merchants brought stories of giant reptiles, authors might place them in their works alongside well-documented species. This mix of fact and myth contributed to the persistent belief that actual dragons might exist somewhere in the far reaches of the known world.

### Dragons in Poetry and Allegory
Roman poets, such as Ovid in his *Metamorphoses*, included transformations that involved serpents or draconic imagery. Sometimes, a god would punish a mortal by turning them into a serpent. Elsewhere, a serpent might represent cunning, danger, or doom. Though not all of these references describe "dragons" in the strict sense, the broader serpentine symbolism fed into the cultural fascination with reptilian monsters.

# CHAPTER FOUR: DRAGONS IN NORTHERN EUROPEAN LORE

## Introduction

Northern Europe developed its own dragon lore, drawing partly from older Indo-European myths and partly from local beliefs about serpents and monsters. Early Celtic and Germanic tribes told stories of great worm-like creatures, while Norse mythology introduced cosmic serpents that threatened the balance of the world. Over time, these tales grew to include dragons that guarded treasure hoards, demanded tribute, or battled gods and heroes.

In this chapter, we will explore how dragons appeared in the myths and legends of the Celts, Germanic peoples, and Norse cultures. We will look at famous examples like Fafnir, Nidhogg, and Jormungandr, along with lesser-known creatures. We will also see how early Anglo-Saxon works—most notably *Beowulf*—featured formidable dragons that shaped heroic narratives. Though the medieval period would later develop the concept of the dragon even further, here we focus on the foundations laid by Northern European lore in its earlier stages.

---

## 1. Early Celtic Myths and Serpents

The Celtic world once spanned across Gaul (modern France), the British Isles, and parts of Central Europe. Though much of ancient Celtic culture is known through later Roman or Christian sources, we can still piece together some glimpses of serpent or dragon-like figures. The Celts revered nature and often gave animals spiritual significance. Snakes, in particular, could represent healing, knowledge, or danger, depending on the region and tribe.

**Serpents in Celtic Art**
Archaeological finds show stylized serpents carved into jewelry, weapons, and stones. These often have intertwined, looping bodies, a style that later became common in early medieval Insular art. While it is not always clear if these depictions represent literal snakes or mythical beasts, the emphasis on twisting, elaborate forms suggests a fascination with serpentine imagery.

### Lake and River Monsters

Some Celtic tales spoke of water monsters or serpents lurking in lakes and rivers. The idea of a dangerous creature living underwater might be an early form of what we later think of as a "dragon," especially in the sense of a wyrm or worm-like being. These local legends could vary from one tribe to another, sometimes describing a guardian spirit, sometimes a malevolent force that demanded offerings.

### Transition to Dragon-Like Creatures

As Celtic societies came into contact with the classical world, Greek and Roman writers sometimes labeled these Celtic serpent-monsters as "dragons," since that was the nearest term in their vocabulary. Over centuries, this identification helped blend Celtic serpent-lore with broader European dragon myths. While pure evidence of "dragons" in the earliest Celtic traditions is sparse, the seeds of the concept are there in the form of revered or feared serpents.

---

## 2. The British Isles and the Welsh Dragon Concept

Wales is famous for its dragon emblem in modern times, but the idea of a red dragon connected to Welsh identity has deep historical roots. Some early Welsh tales, possibly derived from older Celtic myths, mention dragons or serpents battling beneath the earth.

### The Prophecy of Two Dragons

A notable story appears in the *Historia Brittonum* (often attributed to Nennius), which tells how King Vortigern tried to build a fortress that kept collapsing. Consulting magicians suggested that two dragons—one red, one white—were fighting under the ground, causing the walls to fall. The red dragon eventually triumphed, representing the Britons, while the white dragon symbolized the Saxons. Though this account is somewhat later (early medieval), it likely has older mythic elements. It also shows how dragons became tied to national or tribal identity.

### Legends of Lake and Cave Dragons

Welsh folklore also features local dragons living in caves or lakes, terrorizing communities until a hero drives them away. Some of these stories might stem from earlier Celtic serpent-lore mixed with later dragon imagery introduced from Roman or Christian influences. Though we have few purely pre-Roman sources for these tales, the recurring motif of a large reptilian beast in the British landscape suggests a longstanding tradition.

## 3. Germanic Tribal Beliefs: The Wyrm and Worm

Early Germanic cultures, spread across what is now Germany, Scandinavia, and parts of Eastern Europe, had their own word for serpent or dragon: *wyrm* (in Old English) or *ormr* (in Old Norse). This term often referred to a snake-like creature, large and fearsome. Unlike some Greek dragons, a wyrm might not have wings, but it was no less terrifying.

**Oral Traditions and Tribal Identity**
Before written records, Germanic tribes passed down their myths orally. Stories of heroes battling monstrous serpents or wyrms were part of the cultural tradition. In many of these tales, the wyrm guarded treasure or demanded tribute. A warrior who overcame such a beast gained glory and riches, establishing his legacy among his people.

**Influence from Roman and Celtic Myths**
As Germanic tribes interacted with the Roman Empire, they may have picked up new ideas about serpents and dragons. Similarly, contact with Celtic groups could have introduced or reinforced beliefs about monstrous worms. Over time, these interactions helped shape a distinct Northern European image of a dragon as a treasure-hoarding, cave-dwelling monster.

## 4. Fafnir: A Cursed Dragon in the Völsunga Saga

One of the most famous dragons in Northern European lore is Fafnir from the *Völsunga saga*, a Norse tale likely compiled in the 13th century but based on older oral traditions. Fafnir was originally a dwarf or a man (the sources vary), who was consumed by greed after obtaining a cursed treasure known as the Andvari's gold. Overcome by avarice and the curse, Fafnir transformed into a dragon to guard his hoard.

### The Story of Sigurd (Siegfried)

Sigurd, a legendary hero, is guided by the god Odin (in some accounts) to slay Fafnir. Using a sword forged from broken pieces of a mighty blade, Sigurd ambushes Fafnir by digging a pit and striking the dragon's underside as it crawls over him. Fafnir's dying words include warnings about the curse and attempts to dissuade Sigurd from taking the gold.

### Symbolism of Greed and Transformation

Fafnir represents the destructive power of greed. The idea that one can physically turn into a dragon due to overwhelming desire highlights a moral lesson: obsession with wealth leads to monstrous outcomes. This theme appears repeatedly in later European tales of dragons jealously guarding treasures.

### Influence on Later Germanic Lore

The story of Fafnir's slaying became a key narrative in the broader Germanic epic tradition, influencing German legends of Siegfried in the *Nibelungenlied*. The image of a cursed dragon, once human, resonates in many later stories, reinforcing the link between dragons and immense treasures.

---

## 5. Nidhogg: The Corpse Gnawer of Norse Myth

Norse cosmology presented a grand vision of the world tree, Yggdrasil, connecting the various realms of gods, humans, giants, and the dead. At the lowest level, in the realm called Niflheim or near Hel's domain, lurks the dragon (or serpent) Nidhogg. Its name translates to something like "Malice Striker" or "Curse Striker."

### Role in the Cosmic Balance

Nidhogg gnaws at the roots of Yggdrasil, threatening the stability of the entire cosmic structure. Meanwhile, an eagle perches at the top of Yggdrasil, and a squirrel named Ratatoskr runs up and down, carrying insults between the eagle and Nidhogg. This myth suggests that conflict and tension exist at all levels of the universe, from lofty heavens to dark underworlds.

### A Symbol of Destruction and Decay

While Nidhogg is not described in lengthy heroic tales, its presence as a force of decay is significant. By gnawing the tree's roots, it slowly undermines the life force that sustains the cosmos. Scholars interpret Nidhogg as a symbol of entropy or the inevitability of destruction. Still, Yggdrasil endures, reflecting the Norse view that chaos and order must coexist until Ragnarok, the final battle of the gods.

**Dragon or Serpent?**
In some translations, Nidhogg is labeled a serpent; in others, a dragon. Norse sources often use terms interchangeably, focusing more on its harmful, devouring nature. Regardless of the label, Nidhogg fits the broad concept of a dragon as a mighty reptilian force endangering cosmic stability.

---

## 6. Jormungandr: The Midgard Serpent

Another colossal serpent in Norse myth is Jormungandr, also called the Midgard Serpent. A child of the trickster god Loki and the giantess Angrboda, Jormungandr was cast into the sea by Odin, where it grew so large that it encircled the entire world (Midgard), biting its own tail.

**Thor's Eternal Foe**
Jormungandr is the arch-enemy of Thor, the thunder god. The Eddic poems describe multiple encounters between them. In one famous episode, Thor goes fishing with the giant Hymir and hooks Jormungandr. The two engage in a ferocious struggle, but Hymir cuts the line before Thor can strike the serpent, allowing it to escape. The final confrontation is prophesied to occur at Ragnarok, where Thor will slay Jormungandr but then die from the serpent's poison.

**Symbolic Meaning**
Like Nidhogg, Jormungandr represents a cosmic threat. By encircling Midgard, it literally holds the world in a loop. The tension between Jormungandr and Thor reflects the broader Norse belief in an inevitable clash between the gods and the forces of chaos. This serpent is often depicted with a dragon-like head and massive coils, making it a prime example of a Northern European dragon archetype—though it remains strongly associated with the sea.

---

## 7. Early Anglo-Saxon References: *Beowulf* and the Dragon

The Anglo-Saxon epic poem *Beowulf* (likely composed between the 8th and 10th centuries) provides one of the earliest detailed dragon narratives in the English tradition. Although this is entering the early medieval period, it still offers a look at how dragons were viewed in Northern European lore that had pre-Christian roots.

### The Dragon's Treasure Hoard
In *Beowulf*, the hero battles a dragon that dwells in a barrow, guarding a vast treasure. An intruder steals a cup from the hoard, prompting the dragon to ravage nearby lands in revenge. This depiction—an aging dragon jealously protecting its gold—became a staple of later stories.

### Beowulf's Final Battle
Beowulf, now an older king, goes to confront the dragon. Though he slays the beast with the help of a young warrior named Wiglaf, he is mortally wounded in the struggle. The poem's climax emphasizes the deadly power of the dragon and the hero's ultimate sacrifice to protect his people.

### Cultural Reflection
The dragon in *Beowulf* stands at the crossroads of pagan and Christian influences, but it is firmly rooted in a Germanic warrior culture that valued bravery in the face of overwhelming odds. The poem's dragon is no misunderstood creature; it is a fearsome threat that must be defeated at great cost. This portrayal would resonate throughout later medieval literature, but its origins lie in older Northern European beliefs about wyrms and monsters.

---

## 8. The Lindworm and Related Creatures

In several Northern European regions, especially in Germanic and Scandinavian folklore, we encounter references to the "lindworm" (or "lindwurm"). A lindworm is typically a two-legged or legless serpent-like dragon. Sometimes it has a pair of front legs but no hind legs, giving it an elongated, worm-like appearance.

### Common Themes
Lindworms often appear in tales of knights or heroes traveling through forests or remote lands. The creature might plague a kingdom until a champion manages to defeat it. In some legends, the lindworm is a cursed prince or a shape-shifting being, echoing the theme of transformation found in the Fafnir myth.

**Connections to Heraldry**

Later medieval heraldry (beyond the scope of this chapter) would feature lindworms in coats of arms. However, the notion of a large serpent with partial limbs likely has older roots. The term "lind" in Old Norse or Old English can mean "serpent" or be linked to dragons. Thus, the lindworm concept reflects another variation of the Northern European dragon, shaped by regional storytelling and folklore.

---

## 9. Symbolic Roles of Dragons in Early Northern Europe

In these pre- or early-medieval Northern European narratives, dragons served multiple symbolic roles:

1. **Guardians of Treasure**: Like Fafnir and the dragon in *Beowulf*, they hoard gold or magical items, representing both wealth and greed.
2. **Forces of Cosmic Destruction**: As with Nidhogg and Jormungandr, they threaten the stability of the world, signifying chaos beneath the surface of reality.
3. **Adversaries for Heroes**: Slaying a dragon was the ultimate test of valor and skill, granting the hero fame and a lasting legacy.
4. **Manifestations of Curses or Transformation**: Fafnir and certain lindworm tales show that dragons can be the result of a curse, warning listeners about moral failings like greed.

These roles underscore how dragons were not merely mindless monsters; they carried deep cultural and spiritual weight, shaped by each society's fears, values, and cosmological views.

---

## 10. Archaeological Clues and Artistic Depictions

While many of these stories survive through written sagas, epics, and legends, archaeology also offers some glimpses into early Northern European dragon imagery:

- **Runestones**: Some runestones, especially in Sweden, show serpentine shapes wrapped around the edges, sometimes interpreted as dragons or snakes providing a protective or commemorative function.

- **Decorated Weapons**: Sword hilts, shields, and helmets occasionally featured stylized beast heads. Although not always labeled as dragons, the serpent-like or draconic style suggests a symbolic link.
- **Carvings on Wood and Stone**: Norse and Germanic artists used intricate knotwork featuring animal forms, including serpents. The same swirling patterns that once were purely ornamental might also reflect mythical beasts in a coded or symbolic way.

These art forms do not usually provide direct narratives, but they show that the idea of serpentine creatures was widespread. The distinction between a mere snake and a "dragon" might not have been rigid in every case, but the presence of powerful, twisting reptilian figures in art indicates a deep cultural fascination.

---

## 11. Oral vs. Written Traditions and the Evolution of Dragon Myths

One reason Northern European dragon lore is so varied is that much of it comes from oral tradition. These tales changed as they were retold through generations, only later being written down in sagas, poems, and chronicles. By the time a story was recorded, it might have absorbed influences from neighboring cultures or from newly introduced religions like Christianity.

- **Blending with Christian Themes**: As Christianity spread through Northern Europe, scribes who wrote down older myths might have altered dragon stories to reflect Christian morality. Dragons could be portrayed as embodiments of sin or agents of the devil. This is more pronounced in medieval texts but may have begun in earlier transitional periods.
- **Loss and Fragmentation**: Many Germanic tales have survived only in partial form, so we might only see hints of a once-rich dragon tradition. Archetypal stories—such as the hero's confrontation with a dragon—remain, but other details have been lost to time.

Despite these challenges, the core image of a fearsome serpent or wyrm, guarding treasure or threatening cosmic order, persisted. This continuity suggests that the dragon archetype was powerful and meaningful to the people of Northern Europe well before written histories.

# CHAPTER FIVE: THE DRAGONS OF THE FAR EAST

## Introduction

Among all the cultural traditions in which dragons appear, those of the Far East—especially China, Korea, Japan, and parts of Southeast Asia—are some of the most distinctive and enduring. Far Eastern dragons differ markedly from their Western counterparts. While Western tales often depict dragons as malevolent, treasure-hoarding beasts, Eastern dragons are frequently regarded as wise, benevolent, and closely connected with nature's forces.

In this chapter, we will explore the historical roots of Far Eastern dragons. We begin with ancient Chinese civilization, where dragons (called *long* or *lung* in Mandarin) became symbols of imperial power and cosmic harmony. Then we look at how these ideas spread and developed in places like Korea and Japan. We will also note the presence of dragon-like beings in Southeast Asia, where serpentine water spirits known as Nagas and related figures influenced local beliefs. By examining these foundational myths and early texts, we discover how Far Eastern dragons came to represent concepts of authority, wisdom, and balance.

---

## 1. Early Chinese Dragon Myths and Archaeological Evidence

### 1.1 The Place of Dragons in Ancient Chinese Culture

The oldest evidence for dragons in China appears around the time of the Neolithic era. Archaeologists have found jade carvings and pottery fragments from as early as the Hongshan Culture (about 4700–2900 BCE) that depict curved, serpentine forms. While these may not be "dragons" in the modern sense, many scholars believe they represent proto-dragons. These early artifacts often show a creature with a sinuous, snake-like body, sometimes with a head reminiscent of a pig or horse.

By the time of the Shang dynasty (circa 1600–1046 BCE), the Chinese dragon was firmly entrenched in religious practices. Oracle bone inscriptions—used for divination—make references to creatures that may have been dragons, suggesting an already well-developed notion of powerful reptilian spirits. In these inscriptions, the dragon often appears as an ally of the king, invoked in rituals for rain or good harvests.

## 1.2 The Cosmic Dragon and Nature

In the Chinese conception, dragons were strongly associated with water, whether as controllers of rain or guardians of rivers and seas. Unlike the Western notion of a fire-breathing beast, the classic Chinese dragon governed storms, symbolizing fertility and abundance. This association with water and life-giving rain made the dragon a positive force in agricultural societies.

Furthermore, Chinese dragons were sometimes linked to the idea of cosmic order. In the later Zhou dynasty (1046–256 BCE) and subsequent periods, dragons were seen as part of the balance between Heaven and Earth. Literature from this era begins to emphasize the dragon's role as a mediator between gods and humans, bridging the spiritual and physical realms.

---

# 2. Dragons in Early Chinese Literature and Philosophy

## 2.1 The "Classic of Mountains and Seas"

One of the oldest Chinese texts mentioning strange creatures, including serpentine beings, is the *Shan Hai Jing* (山海经), or "Classic of Mountains and Seas." Compiled over centuries (some parts possibly dating back to the Zhou dynasty or earlier), this text describes various mythic landscapes and creatures. While it does not always use the modern word for dragon (*long*), it includes references to serpents or reptilian monsters that can transform. These beings often guard sacred places, echoing universal themes of dragons as gatekeepers to forbidden knowledge or treasures.

## 2.2 Confucian and Daoist Views

During the Spring and Autumn (770–476 BCE) and Warring States (475–221 BCE) periods, two major schools of thought—Confucianism and Daoism—took shape. Although these philosophies did not revolve around dragons, they often used dragon symbolism to represent virtue, transformation, or heavenly favor. Confucian texts sometimes likened the sage or the noble person to a dragon rising toward the sky—a metaphor for moral and intellectual excellence.

In Daoist thought, dragons were seen as powerful embodiments of *qi* (vital energy) and natural forces. They could fly through the clouds or dive into the depths of the sea, moving freely between realms. The famous Daoist philosopher Zhuangzi used the image of a dragon to illustrate the concept of effortless action and the boundless potential of spiritual freedom.

### 2.3 Historical Records
By the Han dynasty (206 BCE–220 CE), historical writers like Sima Qian began to compile extensive works that mentioned dragons in both mythic and semi-historical contexts. The *Records of the Grand Historian* includes accounts of emperors who claimed dragon ancestry or performed rituals to honor dragon deities. These references demonstrate how deeply woven dragons were into the political and cultural tapestry of China.

---

## 3. The Dragon as Symbol of Imperial Authority

### 3.1 Origins of the Imperial Dragon
The concept of the emperor as the "Son of Heaven" took shape during the Zhou dynasty and was solidified under the Han. Because the dragon was already associated with Heaven, rain, and prosperity, linking the imperial throne with dragon symbolism was natural. Emperors adopted the dragon as their personal emblem, stitching it onto robes, decorating palace walls, and sculpting it in official seals.

### 3.2 The Nine Dragon Motif
Later dynasties, particularly the Tang (618–907 CE) and Song (960–1279 CE), developed elaborate dragon imagery for court usage. The "Nine Dragons" motif—a set of stylized dragons—became popular in imperial art. Each dragon represented different powers or cosmic elements, reinforcing the notion that the emperor commanded the forces of nature.

### 3.3 The Forbidden Association
Over time, it became illegal for anyone other than the emperor to display a five-clawed dragon (the highest form of the imperial dragon) on clothing or possessions. Lesser forms (four-clawed or three-clawed dragons) could be used by nobility or officials, but the five-clawed dragon was restricted to imperial

usage. Violating this rule could result in severe punishment, underlining how the dragon was a tangible statement of authority.

### 3.4 Imperial Ceremonies and Dragon Worship
Chinese emperors performed grand rituals involving dragon dances or offerings to dragon gods for favorable weather. At times of drought or flood, the court appealed to these divine dragon spirits to restore balance. The emperor's role as a mediator between Heaven and Earth underscored the importance of dragons in legitimizing and maintaining dynastic power.

---

## 4. Dragons in Early Chinese Folklore and Legend

### 4.1 Tales of Dragon Kings
Popular folklore introduced the concept of "Dragon Kings" (龙王), each ruling a sea or major body of water. These Dragon Kings were anthropomorphic beings capable of taking human form, yet they retained their dragon essence. Fishermen, farmers, and travelers prayed to them for calm seas or timely rains. Stories told of humans visiting underwater dragon palaces, where the Dragon King might bestow gifts or demand restitution for human misdeeds.

### 4.2 White Dragons and Black Dragons
Chinese stories often differentiated dragon colors to signify their nature. White dragons, for instance, might be omens of a significant change or event. Black dragons could represent storms and fierce tempests. Though color symbolism varied by region, the idea that dragons had distinct personalities, powers, and moral inclinations was common in popular tales.

### 4.3 Human-Dragon Transformations
A recurring theme in Chinese lore involves individuals transforming into dragons after achieving spiritual insight or performing great acts of virtue. In one story, a scholar obtains the secret of immortality and becomes a dragon, ascending to the heavens. This motif suggests that the dragon form is the pinnacle of spiritual power, reflecting Chinese beliefs in transformation and transcendence.

---

## 5. Dragons in Korea: The Yong and Imugi

### 5.1 Early Korean Dragon Lore
Korean culture inherited many ideas from China, including the concept of dragons as benevolent, water-related spirits. In Korean, the dragon is called *yong* (용). Like the Chinese dragon, the *yong* is often a symbol of royalty, good fortune, and power over natural forces.

### 5.2 The Imugi: Proto-Dragons
A unique Korean twist is the *imugi* (이무기), a lesser dragon or serpent said to be in training to become a full-fledged dragon. According to legend, an *imugi* is a giant serpent that must earn its transformation by performing virtuous deeds or receiving heavenly favor. If successful, it ascends to heaven and becomes a true dragon. This idea reinforces the notion that dragons are not merely monsters but exalted beings that can evolve spiritually.

### 5.3 Mythical Kings and Dragon Ancestry
Several ancient Korean kingdoms claimed descent from dragon-like beings. For instance, in some Goryeo (918–1392 CE) era tales, founding rulers had miraculous births involving dragons or dragon eggs. These stories helped legitimize royal lines, just as in China. Archaeological finds, such as royal tombs decorated with dragon motifs, highlight the significance of the dragon as a regal and divine emblem.

### 5.4 Connection to Rain and Agriculture
Similar to Chinese beliefs, Korean dragons were invoked in rain-making ceremonies. During droughts, local temples or shrines might hold rites to appease the dragon spirits. Folk traditions often involved chanting, dancing, and the burning of incense, reflecting a community's hope that the dragons would bring beneficial weather.

---

## 6. Dragons in Early Japan: Tatsu and Ryū

### 6.1 Ancient Japanese Beliefs
Japanese dragon lore, like Korea's, was influenced by Chinese culture and myth but also retained indigenous elements from the Shinto tradition. In Japanese, dragons are commonly known as *tatsu* or *ryū* (竜/龍). References to serpentine

deities appear in the Kojiki (712 CE) and Nihon Shoki (720 CE), two early chronicles of Japanese mythology and history.

## 6.2 Yamata no Orochi

One of the most famous dragon-like creatures in ancient Japanese myth is Yamata no Orochi, an eight-headed serpent. According to the Kojiki, the storm god Susanoo encountered Orochi terrorizing a local family by demanding the sacrifice of their daughters. Susanoo tricked the serpent into drinking strong wine, then killed it while it was inebriated. The myth ends with Susanoo finding a legendary sword in one of Orochi's tails—a recurring motif of precious items hidden within dragons.

## 6.3 Water Deities and Dragons

Many Shinto deities linked with water or rain have dragon aspects. Ryūjin or Watatsumi, for example, is a sea god portrayed as a dragon residing in an underwater palace. Like the Chinese Dragon Kings, Ryūjin controlled tides and storms. Fishermen and sailors prayed to him for safe voyages. Legends speak of humans visiting Ryūjin's palace or receiving magical jewels that control the seas.

## 6.4 Dragons and the Imperial Family

In some versions of Japanese mythology, the imperial family descends from deities connected to dragons or serpentine forms, paralleling Chinese and Korean legends. While the direct claim to dragon ancestry is not as pronounced as in Chinese imperial culture, the association between dragons and imperial rule exists in subtle ways through art, regalia, and court ceremonies.

---

# 7. Dragons in Early Southeast Asia

## 7.1 The Naga Tradition

Though "Naga" is a Sanskrit term commonly associated with South Asia, it also plays a significant role in the mythologies of Burma (Myanmar), Thailand, Laos, and Cambodia. In these regions, Nagas are powerful serpent beings that often dwell in rivers and underground realms. They can shape-shift into human form, and in many legends, they are guardians of fertility, wealth, and royal lineages.

## 7.2 Local Adaptations

Each Southeast Asian culture has adapted the Naga to its environment and local beliefs. For example:

- **In Thailand**, Nagas appear on temple stairways, symbolizing protection and a connection to the underworld.
- **In Laos**, the Mekong River is said to be home to many Nagas, which are celebrated in festivals and legends about their origin.
- **In Cambodia**, stories describe Nagas as the original inhabitants of the land, marrying into human royalty and ensuring prosperity.

Though these beings are more often called "Nagas" rather than "dragons," their serpentine shape and supernatural abilities place them in the broad category of dragon-like creatures in Far Eastern and Southeast Asian folklore.

**7.3 Rain, Rivers, and Royalty**
As in China, dragons or serpentine spirits in Southeast Asia are strongly tied to water. Communities living along major rivers rely on them for agriculture, trade, and sustenance, so it makes sense that a revered mythical serpent or dragon would emerge as a protective deity. Rulers might claim a special relationship with these beings, further legitimizing their control over the land and its resources.

---

## 8. Dragons and Society: Rituals, Festivals, and Symbolism

**8.1 Dragon Dances and Celebrations (Historical Context)**
While dragon dances are often seen in later dynastic and even modern contexts, the roots go back centuries. Historical documents from the Han and Tang periods reference large-scale celebrations that included processions featuring dragon effigies. These displays were meant to placate or honor dragon spirits, especially during key agricultural festivals.

**8.2 Temple Offerings**
In many parts of East and Southeast Asia, local temples or shrines dedicated to dragons or water spirits collected offerings from citizens seeking good fortune. Rituals might include burning incense, chanting prayers, or releasing paper effigies into rivers. These practices reinforced a communal bond, as everyone relied on dragon blessings for rainfall, bountiful harvests, or safe voyages.

**8.3 Dragon Imagery in Daily Life**
Dragons also appeared on everyday objects—ceramics, textiles, and jewelry. While the highest forms of dragon iconography were reserved for royalty (as in

imperial China), simpler dragon motifs were common among merchants and commoners. For example, a fisherman might paint a dragon on his boat's prow, believing it would ward off storms.

---

## 9. Moral and Philosophical Aspects of Far Eastern Dragons

### 9.1 Benevolence vs. Fear
Contrary to many Western tales that cast dragons as evil or menacing, Far Eastern dragons often embody benevolence. They bring rain, bestow blessings, and represent good fortune. However, they can become wrathful if disrespected, causing floods or droughts. Thus, the dragon demands respect and proper conduct, reflecting the moral dimension in Chinese, Korean, and Japanese stories.

### 9.2 Confucian Virtue
Dragons in Confucian contexts sometimes symbolize the virtuous ruler who nurtures the people, just as a dragon nurtures the land with rain. The wise leader, like a dragon, has the power to preserve harmony but must govern ethically to maintain Heaven's mandate. This dual capacity for creation or destruction underscores the moral obligations of those in power.

### 9.3 Daoist and Buddhist Transformations
In Daoist alchemy and spiritual practices, the dragon can represent transformation and immortality. In some Buddhist traditions that reached East Asia, dragons became protectors of the Buddha's teachings, appearing in sutras as wise, enlightened beings. They might hold sacred relics or reveal hidden knowledge. Such stories elevate the dragon to a cosmic guardian, reinforcing religious ideals of compassion and wisdom.

---

## 10. Legacy and Evolution of Far Eastern Dragon Myths

### 10.1 Spread and Adaptation
As different dynasties rose and fell in China, as Korea's kingdoms unified or split, and as Japan shifted from clan-based governance to imperial rule, the dragon myth adapted to new social and political realities. Yet it remained central to

cultural identity. Through trade routes, migration, and conquest, elements of Far Eastern dragon lore also reached neighboring regions, blending with local serpent traditions.

## 10.2 Influence on Neighboring Cultures
Historically, Chinese influence was strong across East Asia. Regions like Vietnam, once part of the Chinese sphere, incorporated dragon symbolism into their royal crests. Japan and Korea also maintained extensive scholarly and diplomatic exchanges with China, adopting certain dragon motifs while retaining their indigenous myths. Southeast Asian societies, similarly, merged Indian Naga lore with Chinese-style dragons, resulting in unique regional variations.

## 10.3 Transition to Later Periods
The Song and Yuan dynasties in China (10th to 14th centuries), the Goryeo and Joseon dynasties in Korea (10th to early 20th centuries), and the Heian and Kamakura periods in Japan (8th to 14th centuries) each saw evolutions in dragon iconography. Though we are avoiding modern history, it is important to note that by the late medieval era, the imagery of the dragon had become even more sophisticated, tied to court rituals, temple art, and popular festivals. All of these developments rested on the ancient foundations described throughout this chapter.

# CHAPTER SIX: DRAGONS IN THE MIDDLE EAST AND NORTH AFRICA

## Introduction

The Middle East and North Africa are lands with deep mythological roots, bridging ancient civilizations like the Persians, Arabs, Phoenicians, and Berbers, along with the vast spread of Semitic cultures. We have already looked at some aspects of Mesopotamian and Egyptian dragon lore in earlier chapters. However, there are many additional stories of dragon-like beings in regions such as Persia, the Arabian Peninsula, the Levant (beyond the earliest references), and North Africa west of Egypt. These myths evolved over centuries, often shaped by Zoroastrian, Jewish, Christian, and eventually Islamic influences.

In this chapter, we explore the older historical and mythic traditions of dragons and serpents that emerged in the Middle East and North Africa. We focus on how these creatures represented chaos, protection, or cosmic strife in different cultural and religious settings. We also look briefly at how these ideas mingled with Greek, Roman, and Near Eastern concepts as empires rose and fell. By concentrating on pre-modern eras, we will see how beliefs about dragons—often called by various local terms—took hold in deserts, oases, and trade routes, carrying echoes of older Mesopotamian serpent lore alongside distinct regional characteristics.

---

## 1. Persian Mythology: Azhi Dahāka (Zahhak) and Dragons

### 1.1 Zoroastrian Roots
Persian dragon lore traces back to the ancient religion of Zoroastrianism, founded by the prophet Zoroaster (Zarathustra) in the second millennium BCE, though exact dates are debated. The holy texts known as the Avesta contain references to dragons or monstrous serpents (*azi*). Chief among these is Azhi Dahāka (modern Persian: Zahhak), a fearsome three-headed dragon or demon that threatened the cosmos.

### 1.2 Azhi Dahāka in the Avesta
In Zoroastrian cosmology, good (Ahura Mazda) battles evil (Angra Mainyu). Azhi

Dahāka stands as one of the forces of chaos. Various portions of the Avesta describe it as an immense serpent with supernatural powers, sometimes devouring livestock or spreading pestilence. While it might share some traits with the giant serpents of Mesopotamia, Azhi Dahāka took on its own distinctly Persian identity.

### 1.3 The Shāhnāmeh and Zahhak
By the time of the Sassanian Empire (224–651 CE) and into the early Islamic era, the figure of Azhi Dahāka evolved into "Zahhak" in Persian literature. The epic poem *Shāhnāmeh* (The Book of Kings), composed by the poet Ferdowsi around the 10th century CE, recounts Zahhak as a tyrannical ruler cursed with snakes growing from his shoulders. Though this is a later story, it retains the dragon-serpent essence in a more symbolic, humanized form. Zahhak must feed these snakes human brains, reflecting a monstrous corruption of nature and kingship.

### 1.4 Other Persian Dragon-Like Creatures
Beyond Azhi Dahāka, Persian myths reference other *azi*, or serpentine monsters, lurking in remote mountains or deserts. Heroic figures like Rostam often face reptilian foes, underscoring the ongoing theme of cosmic or moral conflict. The dragon is not merely a beast; it is a living expression of disorder that must be contained by heroic virtue.

---

## 2. Pre-Islamic Arabian Serpents and Dragons

### 2.1 Desert Legends
Before the advent of Islam in the 7th century CE, the Arabian Peninsula had a rich tapestry of oral traditions. Tribes spoke of monstrous serpents in desert caves or oases. These could be giant vipers, pythons, or purely mythical creatures that swallowed camels whole. With limited water sources, a fierce serpent controlling a well or spring would become a natural focal point of dread and storytelling.

### 2.2 Jinn and Serpents
While the concept of *jinn* (supernatural beings) is central to Islamic tradition, pre-Islamic Arab societies also recognized spirits that dwelt in isolated places. Some were described as serpentine or shape-shifting, blending the idea of a jinn

with a dragon-like creature. Though not often referred to as "dragons" in the strict sense, these beings shared the fearsome qualities of reptilian monsters.

### 2.3 Tribal Epics and Poetry
Pre-Islamic Arabic poetry (the Mu'allaqāt and other collections) rarely features full dragon narratives but does employ serpentine imagery to convey danger or cunning. A poet might describe an enemy warrior as striking "like a desert serpent," hinting at lethal speed or hidden power. While such references are brief, they contribute to an overall cultural image of the serpent as a formidable foe.

---

## 3. Dragons and Serpents in Early Jewish Traditions (Beyond the Biblical Leviathan)

### 3.1 Post-Biblical Writings
In Chapter Two, we touched on the biblical creature Leviathan, often described as a monstrous sea serpent or dragon. Later Jewish texts, including some parts of the Talmud and midrashic literature (rabbinic commentaries), expand on serpent-like creatures. They reframe Leviathan and similar beasts in moral or eschatological terms, focusing on the End of Days when God slays these chaos monsters for the righteous to feast upon.

### 3.2 Behemoth, Leviathan, and Rahab
Though Behemoth is generally a land monster and Leviathan is aquatic, some traditions mention a creature called Rahab, associated with primeval waters. While not strictly labeled a dragon, it aligns with the concept of a serpentine chaos being. Ancient Jewish thought, influenced by older Near Eastern myths, often saw these monstrous forces as part of God's plan—created to test or eventually showcase divine power.

### 3.3 Symbolic Interpretations
By the Hellenistic and Roman periods, Jewish scholars in places like Alexandria blended Greek philosophical ideas with traditional beliefs. Dragons or serpents thus became allegories for sin, foreign oppression, or cosmic chaos. While these references appear mostly in religious and exegetical works rather than epics, they contribute to the broader Middle Eastern tapestry of serpentine lore.

## 4. Greco-Roman Influence in the Levant and North Africa

### 4.1 Cultural Syncretism
After Alexander the Great's conquests (late 4th century BCE), much of the Middle East and Egypt fell under Hellenistic rule, later absorbed by Rome. Dragons in the Greek and Roman sense—like drakons or sea serpents—began to merge with local beliefs. Egyptian temples built under Ptolemaic rule, for instance, might show serpent gods in a Greek-influenced artistic style.

### 4.2 Serapis and Hybrid Deities
Serapis, a syncretic god introduced by the Ptolemies in Egypt, combined aspects of Greek and Egyptian religion. Although not depicted as a dragon, Serapis's cult sometimes included serpent symbolism, reflecting the broader Hellenistic fascination with reptilian icons. Meanwhile, older Egyptian serpent deities like Apophis or the uraeus cobra retained their local importance but were reinterpreted under Greek dominion.

### 4.3 Roman Africa and Carthaginian Traces
Further west, in the territory once held by Carthage (modern Tunisia), Roman occupation led to new cultural blends. Carthaginians themselves had earlier Phoenician roots, meaning the region already possessed serpent or sea-monster traditions akin to those of the Levant. Under Rome, classic "draco" motifs appeared in military and official settings. Local altars and mosaics sometimes showed serpents or dragons as protective spirits or boundary markers.

---

## 5. North African Berber and Libyan Myths

### 5.1 Ancient Berber Beliefs
The Berber peoples (also known as Amazigh) inhabit vast regions of North Africa, from Morocco to Libya. Tracing their myths can be difficult due to limited written records in ancient times. However, Greek and Roman authors occasionally mention local legends of giant serpents in the mountains or deserts of Libya and Mauretania (an ancient region of North Africa).

### 5.2 The "Libyan Serpent" in Greek Sources
Greek stories sometimes referred to certain desert areas as home to monstrous serpents so large they could challenge entire armies. Although these accounts

may be exaggerated traveler's tales, they contributed to the image of North Africa as a land where giant serpents or dragon-like creatures lurked. Herodotus and Diodorus Siculus mention serpent-infested deserts, linking them to the goddess Athena's origins in "Libya" (according to one variant myth).

### 5.3 Local Guardian Spirits
Some Berber communities practiced forms of animism that included reptilian guardian spirits. These might be tied to water sources—an oasis or a hidden spring. While less documented, oral traditions in the Atlas Mountains or Saharan oases occasionally reference serpents that watch over caves or rare wells. This notion parallels Middle Eastern desert myths of well-guarding serpents.

---

## 6. Later Transformations Under Islamic Influence (Pre-Modern Period)

### 6.1 Early Islamic Attitudes
With the rise of Islam in the 7th century CE, many older myths were reinterpreted. The Quran itself does not mention "dragons" explicitly but does include references to serpents, such as the staff of Moses turning into a snake. Over time, Islamic folklore would incorporate and adapt local serpent-lore, sometimes labeling monstrous creatures as *marids* (a type of powerful jinn) or using broader Arabic terms for dragons (*tinnīn, thu'bān*, etc.).

### 6.2 Persian and Arab Folktales
In Persian cultural regions, older Zoroastrian tales of Azhi Dahāka or other serpents were woven into Islamic-era stories. For instance, medieval Persian romances might feature a hero battling a *tinnīn* in remote mountains. Arab storytellers in regions like the Levant or Hijaz also told folktales of monstrous serpents, mixing tribal lore with Islamic moral lessons. These narratives typically upheld heroic virtues such as faith, courage, and devotion, pitted against cunning reptilian foes.

### 6.3 The Spread of "Dragon" Terms
Trade routes across the Middle East and North Africa facilitated the exchange of stories. Merchants might hear about Far Eastern dragons from Chinese traders along the Silk Road, while also encountering local Persian or Arabian serpent myths. Over time, the term "dragon" (in Greek and Latin forms) merged with

local words, creating a linguistic web of references. By the high medieval period, Arabic texts occasionally used both local and borrowed terms to describe large serpents or mythical dragons.

---

## 7. Dragons in Middle Eastern Art and Architecture (Pre-Modern)

### 7.1 Decorative Motifs
Though more common in East Asia, dragon motifs also appear in Middle Eastern artifacts. For example, some Seljuk-era (11th–13th centuries) pottery and metalwork from Persia and Anatolia show stylized winged serpents or dragons chasing one another in circular patterns. These designs likely reflect a mix of Chinese influence (via the Silk Road) and local interpretations of fearsome beasts.

### 7.2 Islamic Calligraphy and Dragons
In a few medieval Islamic manuscripts, especially those dealing with cosmology or bestiaries, artists integrated dragons into elaborate calligraphic frames. The serpent or dragon might loop around the text, signifying the all-encompassing nature of God's creation. While less overtly religious than direct Quranic art (which avoids anthropomorphic or zoomorphic depictions of divine subjects), these manuscripts display a fascination with mythical beasts within an Islamic cultural sphere.

### 7.3 Architectural Elements
Carvings on mosques or palaces rarely feature dragons outright, given the general aniconic tradition in Islamic art. However, secular structures—like caravanserais or fortresses—sometimes included decorative stone reliefs of serpentine creatures, particularly in regions where pre-Islamic traditions lingered (Persia, Central Asia, or certain parts of the Levant). These might symbolize protection or intimidation, drawing on older motifs of the dragon as a guardian.

---

## 8. Dragon-Like Tales Along the Sahara and Red Sea Coasts

### 8.1 Travelers' Reports
Medieval geographers and travelers, such as Ibn Battuta or earlier explorers,

recorded local legends of monstrous serpents in the Sahara or along the Red Sea coasts. Some tales likely stem from encounters with large pythons or crocodiles, magnified by rumor. Over time, these stories fed the idea of "dragons" inhabiting remote deserts, an echo of earlier Greek and Roman accounts of North African serpents.

## 8.2 Cross-Cultural Influences

The Red Sea region was a crossroads for African, Arabian, and even South Asian merchants. Over the centuries, it is plausible that myths of Ethiopian or Somali "dragons"—actually giant snakes or foreign accounts of crocodiles—blended with Arabian traditions of desert-dwelling serpents. This ongoing cultural exchange contributed to the diversity of serpentine lore in the broader Middle East and North Africa.

---

# 9. The Symbolic Role of Dragons in Middle Eastern and North African Societies

## 9.1 Cosmic Chaos and Divine Power

Like in Mesopotamian mythology, serpentine or dragon-like beings frequently symbolize chaos or primeval disorder. Whether it is Azhi Dahāka in Persia, Leviathan in Hebrew tradition, or desert serpents in Arabian lore, these beasts often mark the boundary between human civilization and untamed forces. Confrontation with a dragon thus represents confronting existential threats—be they moral, environmental, or social.

## 9.2 Guardians of Treasure or Water

Guarding water sources is a recurring theme in arid lands. Since water is so precious in deserts and semi-deserts, the idea of a dragon or giant serpent controlling a spring or oasis is powerful. Heroes who triumph over such a beast free the water for their community, a direct parallel to the "treasure-guarding dragon" motif found worldwide.

## 9.3 Moral Lessons

In many stories, the dragon or serpent becomes a test of character. The hero must demonstrate faith, courage, or cunning to succeed. Alternatively, a ruler who fails to appease or defeat a serpent might be deemed unfit to govern. These moral dimensions highlight the enduring role of dragon-like myths as teaching tools and reflections of societal values.

## 10. Lesser-Known Regional Variations

### 10.1 Phoenician Vestiges
Along the Levantine coast, where the ancient Phoenicians once thrived, we find occasional references to sea serpents that threatened ships or harbors. Over centuries, these might blend with Greek-based sea dragon tales—like the monster sent by Poseidon in the myth of Andromeda (though that is typically placed near Ethiopia, the motif traveled widely).

### 10.2 Ethiopian Highlands
Ethiopia, while just outside North Africa geographically, has old legends of serpent-like creatures in ravines and highland lakes. Some Christian Ethiopian texts, influenced by biblical motifs, describe monstrous serpents reminiscent of Leviathan or Behemoth. Travelers' accounts from the medieval period mention these legends, though details are sparse.

### 10.3 Berber and Tuareg Stories
Among Tuareg or other Saharan Berber groups, the *iginaden* or serpent spirits sometimes appear in folktales. However, documentation is limited. These serpents can cause or cure sickness, echoing the broader Middle Eastern idea that serpents are guardians of hidden power—water, knowledge, or healing.

## 11. Echoes of Older Civilizations in Pre-Modern Times

### 11.1 Continuity of Themes
Across the Middle East and North Africa, older themes from Mesopotamian, Egyptian, and Persian lore did not vanish when new empires or religions arose. Instead, they persisted in folk traditions, local stories, and sometimes in the official culture of new ruling classes. The idea of the serpentine dragon as a foe of the gods (or of a rightful king) remained an undercurrent throughout the centuries.

## 11.2 Interaction with Greek and Roman Influences

Hellenistic and Roman presences introduced classical dragon images, but local cultures adapted them, creating hybrids that might bear the name "drakon" yet behave like an Arabian desert serpent or a Persian *azi*. By late antiquity, the Middle East was a patchwork of mythic references, each shaped by environment, politics, and faith.

## 11.3 Religious Reinterpretation

Jewish, Christian, and Islamic traditions each reframed older dragon myths. In some cases, these religions demonized the dragon as an embodiment of evil or sin. In others, they recast the serpent as a test of divine power. Over time, each faith developed its own symbolic relationship with serpents and dragons, adding layers of moral and eschatological meaning.

# CHAPTER SEVEN: DRAGONS ACROSS SUB-SAHARAN AFRICA

## Introduction

Sub-Saharan Africa covers a vast region south of the Sahara Desert. This expanse includes numerous cultures, languages, and environments—from the Sahel and savannas in the north to tropical rainforests in central Africa and temperate highlands in the south. Given this immense diversity, there is no single, unified concept of the "dragon" across the region. Instead, we find a wide array of serpent-like beings, water spirits, and reptilian creatures in different local traditions.

In many cases, these beings do not precisely match the image of the winged, fire-breathing dragon known in much of Eurasia. Instead, Sub-Saharan African myths often speak of massive snakes or water-dwelling monsters that control rivers, lakes, rainfall, or healing powers. These creatures sometimes blend with the concept of ancestral spirits or deities, reflecting local religious beliefs about the interplay between the natural and supernatural worlds.

This chapter explores some of the major dragon-like entities and large serpent myths found across Sub-Saharan Africa. We begin by looking at West African legends of water spirits and snake deities, then move to Central Africa's lake monsters and serpentine guardians, followed by East African myths about giant reptiles inhabiting rivers and coastlines, and finally turn to Southern Africa, where stories of cave-dwelling serpents or lightning-linked reptilian beings appear. Throughout, we will see how these creatures connect to concerns about water, fertility, social order, and the thin boundary between the living and the spirit realms.

---

## 1. The Challenge of Defining "Dragons" in an African Context

### 1.1 Different Forms of Serpentine Creatures
When outsiders think of dragons, they often picture a scaled beast with wings, horns, and the ability to breathe fire. In Sub-Saharan Africa, many societies speak instead of giant serpents that can be many times larger than a normal

snake. Some have mythical features—such as bright plumage, luminous scales, or the power to shape-shift into human form. Others dwell primarily in water, controlling rainfall or fish stocks. These creatures might be labeled "dragons" by analogy, though local names and concepts can be quite distinct.

## 1.2 Hybrid Nature of Mythical Snakes

A recurring pattern in African serpent myths is hybridity. A being may appear as a snake but speak with a human voice or carry a spirit's wisdom. In some tales, it can transform into a human, marry among mortals, or demand offerings. Because of this shape-shifting quality, we see repeated themes of crossing boundaries—between water and land, humanity and the supernatural, life and death. Although these traits differ from typical Western "dragon" stories, they serve a similar narrative and symbolic purpose.

## 1.3 Oral Traditions and Regional Variation

Africa's extensive oral traditions mean stories shift from one region to another, shaped by the environment, language, and cultural practices of each community. Myths about serpent-like beasts in a forest region might highlight fertility and healing, while those in semi-arid zones might focus on water scarcity and the importance of controlling a hidden spring. As a result, there is no single "African dragon myth," but rather many localized versions of large serpentine beings fulfilling roles that parallel the dragon archetype seen elsewhere.

---

# 2. West Africa: Water Spirits, Sacred Pythons, and Powerful Serpents

## 2.1 The Cult of the Python (Benin, Togo, and Surrounding Areas)

In parts of West Africa—especially in what is now southern Benin, Togo, and nearby regions—there exists a long history of revering pythons as sacred animals. Vodun (or Voodoo) traditions often include temples dedicated to pythons, which are believed to embody protective deities. Though not typically described as fire-breathing dragons, these large snakes occupy a similar space in the local worldview: they wield tremendous power, demand respect, and can bring both blessings and curses.

Some communities hold festivals in which priests or priestesses handle live pythons, reflecting a deep bond with the serpent spirit. Myths tell of enormous pythons that once protected villages or guided migrations. These pythons might have supernatural attributes—speaking to chosen people, transforming into a human to deliver warnings, or vanishing mysteriously when their task is done.

## 2.2 Mami Wata and the Serpentine Imagery

"Mami Wata," a popular pantheon of water spirits in West and Central Africa, is often depicted with a large snake coiled around her or near her. While Mami Wata is more frequently represented in female human form, the serpent is her companion and symbol. In some stories, the snake is giant and has a dragon-like presence, guarding her underwater realm or punishing those who pollute rivers.

Mami Wata traditions emphasize themes of wealth, sexuality, and healing. The serpent by her side is both a symbol of fertility (connected to water) and a dangerous power that must be approached with care. People seeking Mami Wata's favor might offer gifts at riversides or shrines, hoping for protection, prosperity, or relief from illness. Thus, the serpent stands as both a gateway and guardian, akin to the treasure-guarding dragons in other mythologies.

## 2.3 Guardian Serpents in Forest Regions

In forested parts of Ghana, Côte d'Ivoire, and Nigeria, local myths sometimes describe serpents that watch over hidden groves or sacred waterfalls. These serpents maintain order among forest spirits, ensuring humans do not overexploit resources. A hunter who disrespects the serpent or hunts in a forbidden grove may face misfortune. Stories like these stress the moral relationship between humans and nature, with the serpent embodying the forest's protective wrath.

## 2.4 Serpents in Yoruba Mythology

Among the Yoruba people of southwestern Nigeria, there are numerous deities (Orishas) associated with specific elements. While dragons per se do not feature prominently in Yoruba lore, serpent motifs do appear. For instance, Oshun is a river goddess sometimes accompanied by serpent imagery, symbolizing the meandering flow of water and the hidden dangers beneath a calm surface. Meanwhile, Shango (the deity of thunder and lightning) occasionally battles serpentine spirits linked to storms. These narratives, while distinct from a single "dragon story," contribute to a broader tapestry of African serpent worship or fear.

# 3. Central Africa: Lake Monsters and Serpent Kings

### 3.1 Lake Legends in the Congo Basin
Central Africa's immense Congo Basin, with its dense rainforests and winding rivers, has long been home to tales of water-dwelling monsters. Local communities speak of serpents that inhabit large lakes and underwater caverns. Some stories tell of a colossal snake that only emerges at night, devouring livestock or unlucky travelers who wander too close to the shore.

While these creatures do not always have mythical powers like shapeshifting, they often show uncanny intelligence—evading capture, moving silently, and leaving behind strange tracks or evidence of their presence. In certain traditions, the local chief or a diviner might try to appease the creature with offerings, hoping to secure safe passage for fishing boats and travelers.

### 3.2 Nkisi and Protective Spirits
In parts of modern-day Democratic Republic of the Congo and Angola, the concept of *nkisi* (sacred power objects) includes carved figures or containers said to house spirits. Some are associated with serpent entities that can grant healing or fertility. Like a dragon's lair, the location of an *nkisi* might be a sacred pool or cave guarded by a serpentine guardian.

These guardians can be both beneficial and harmful. If a community respects the sacred site and follows traditional rules, the serpent spirit (or "dragon") protects them from illness, crops failing, or hostile spirits. If they break taboos, the serpent might unleash floods, diseases, or misfortunes. Such beliefs underscore the dynamic tension between humanity and the potent forces symbolized by serpents.

### 3.3 Serpent Kings and Dynastic Legends
Some Central African kingdoms preserved oral histories that mention founding ancestors with serpentine qualities or the ability to communicate with great snakes. Although details vary widely, the overarching theme is that the royal line had a pact with powerful forces of nature, ensuring prosperity and stability for the kingdom. These stories parallel the "dragon kings" of East Asia, except in an African context, the serpentine being is more likely to be a giant python, an anaconda-like creature (in near-rainforest regions), or a legendary snake known by local names.

# 4. East Africa: Coastal Dragons, Nile Serpents, and Inland Myths

### 4.1 Coastal Regions and Swahili Traditions
Along the East African coast, including parts of Kenya, Tanzania, and Mozambique, centuries of trade with Arab merchants introduced new storytelling elements, some referencing dragons or giant serpents called by Arabic-derived terms. Local Swahili lore might feature a monstrous sea snake that terrorizes fishermen, requiring a hero or a powerful spirit to drive it away. Over time, these legends mixed indigenous beliefs with Islamic-inflected ideas of jinn and sea spirits.

### 4.2 The Nile and Great Lakes Region
Moving inland to Uganda, Rwanda, and other Great Lakes territories, we find stories about serpentine creatures lurking in the depths of Lake Victoria, Lake Tanganyika, or Lake Kivu. These might be described as fish-like dragons or serpent spirits that control storms over the water. Fishermen's tales recount sightings of huge aquatic monsters, sometimes endowed with magical properties such as the ability to vanish at will. While modern cryptozoology might label them "lake monsters," local myths treat them as part of a supernatural ecosystem.

### 4.3 Ethiopian Highlands
Though Ethiopia is often considered part of the Horn of Africa and has a distinct cultural history influenced by Christianity since ancient times, older local traditions include references to serpents or serpent-kings. In certain highland communities, legends speak of giant snakes in remote ravines, sometimes linked to older religious beliefs that predate widespread Christianization. These stories, passed down orally, present the serpent as a gatekeeper to hidden knowledge or as a punishment for human arrogance (similar to the role of serpents in other mythologies worldwide).

### 4.4 The Hadimu of Zanzibar
The Hadimu people of Zanzibar (an island off the Tanzanian coast) have tales of giant serpents dwelling in coral caves or undersea grottoes. Such serpents might be placated by annual offerings to ensure smooth ocean currents and good fishing. While not precisely "dragons," these legends echo the concept of a powerful reptilian overlord controlling maritime fortunes.

# 5. Southern Africa: Caves, Lightning, and Rain-Calling Serpents

### 5.1 The "Grootslang" of South African Legend

In parts of South Africa, particularly within Afrikaner and local Bantu-speaking communities, there is a tale of a monstrous serpent or elephant-like beast called the "Grootslang." While the Grootslang legend is partially influenced by colonial-era stories, some strands trace back to older indigenous tales of giant cave-dwelling serpents. The Grootslang is said to live in deep caves or ravines, guarding precious stones—an echo of treasure-hoarding dragons in global mythology.

Though not part of purely pre-colonial tradition in its well-known form, the concept shares traits with older African serpent myths: controlling hidden riches, living underground, and symbolizing an untamed power that can either be appeased or might wreak havoc if disturbed.

### 5.2 Lightning Bird and Serpents

In some Southern African myths, the serpent can be connected to lightning and thunder. For instance, the Zulu tell of the "Lightning Bird" (impundulu), but there are also references to a serpentine force that travels with storms. A lightning strike near a river might be explained by the serpent's wrath. In these stories, serpents have the capacity to bring rain—much like the Far Eastern dragons—though they can also unleash destructive floods or storms.

### 5.3 Serpents of the Great Zimbabwe Ruins

The historical site of Great Zimbabwe (in present-day Zimbabwe) offers limited direct evidence of serpent worship, but local oral traditions mention that powerful spirits—sometimes envisioned as serpentine—protected the city. While stone carvings of actual dragons are not found there, bird and animal motifs appear, leading scholars to speculate about connections to a cult of royal ancestors or protective nature spirits. Some of these spirits may have been described as serpent-like in older legends.

### 5.4 Venda Water Spirits

Among the Venda people of South Africa, water spirits known as *zwidudwane* are sometimes conceived as large serpents dwelling in deep pools. If angered, they cause drownings or water shortages; if appeased, they ensure fish abundance and good harvests. Like many African myths, the story underscores the crucial relationship between humans and water sources. The serpent functions as both a threat and a caretaker—a role resembling dragons in many other cultures.

# 6. Symbolic Roles and Common Themes

### 6.1 Water and Fertility
A unifying theme in many Sub-Saharan African serpent myths is water. In regions where seasonal rainfall is life or death, a creature associated with controlling water resources wields immense power. This is akin to the cosmic dragons of other civilizations that manage rain or rivers. Local customs often require offerings to the serpentine spirit, highlighting a relationship of mutual dependence and respect.

### 6.2 Moral Guardianship
Another common thread is the idea of serpents enforcing moral or social rules. People must not desecrate sacred groves, pollute rivers, or behave disrespectfully toward the spirit's domain. In this way, the serpent or dragon-like being embodies collective values—honoring nature, protecting communal resources, and upholding ancestral traditions.

### 6.3 Healing and Transformative Power
In some West and Central African contexts, serpent spirits are linked to healing and transformation. They can grant knowledge of medicinal plants or cure afflictions if worshippers approach them properly. Occasionally, an individual called by the serpent may become a healer or diviner after a period of seclusion and instruction by the spirit. This transformative aspect aligns with global dragon motifs, where contact with a dragon or serpent often yields hidden wisdom or power.

### 6.4 Boundaries Between Worlds
Sub-Saharan African serpent myths frequently emphasize crossing or guarding boundaries—between land and water, living and dead, mortal and spirit. A serpent might live in a river but appear on land to interact with humans, blurring lines of reality. This power to move between worlds parallels the mythic function of dragons elsewhere as gatekeepers or liminal beings.

---

# 7. Historical Context and Influences

### 7.1 Ancient Contacts and Trade Routes
Throughout Sub-Saharan Africa, trade routes stretching across the Sahara to North Africa, and along the Indian Ocean coast, brought outside ideas that sometimes merged with indigenous serpent lore. Islamic or Arabic tales of

dragons occasionally mingled with local legends, producing new hybrid stories. For instance, the Swahili coast's legends of monstrous sea serpents or jinn-infused dragons reflect centuries of cultural exchange with the Middle East.

### 7.2 Rock Art and Symbolic Evidence
Archaeological evidence for serpent worship or "dragon" imagery in prehistoric Sub-Saharan Africa is scattered. Cave paintings or rock art in the Sahara region (such as the Tassili n'Ajjer in Algeria) and parts of southern Africa (like the Drakensberg paintings) sometimes depict elongated reptilian forms, though it is unclear whether they represent normal snakes, mythic serpents, or purely symbolic shapes. Interpretation remains speculative, but these images could signify that serpentine figures played roles in ritual or myth from ancient times.

### 7.3 Kingdoms and Empires
Powerful African states—such as the Mali Empire, Songhai, Benin Kingdom, Kongo Kingdom, and Great Zimbabwe—each had religious systems that included references to serpents in their cosmic worldview. Royalty might claim a direct link to a serpent deity or keep a sacred python in the royal compound as a living emblem of ancestral power. Although details differ, the association between rulership and serpentine forces suggests parallels to the "imperial dragon" concept seen in other parts of the world.

---

## 8. Encounters with Serpentine Beings in Oral History

### 8.1 Ritual Specialists and Griots
West African griots—oral historians and storytellers—sometimes recount genealogies that include supernatural serpent ancestors or describe heroic battles with monstrous snakes. In East and Central Africa, ritual specialists or diviners may hold knowledge of local serpent legends passed down through apprenticeships. These oral testimonies contain moral lessons, historical claims, and references to treaties with serpent spirits that ensured a community's survival.

### 8.2 Heroic Tales of Serpent Slayers
Though "dragon slayer" narratives in Africa do not always have the same prominence as in medieval Europe, there are local stories of hunters or warriors who kill a menacing giant snake. This feat might establish them as defenders of the community, earn them a new name or status, and prompt celebrations or

songs. Sometimes, the snake's death yields a magical item—perhaps a fang with healing properties or a scale that can ward off evil—resembling the treasure motif seen in worldwide dragon lore.

### 8.3 Interpreting Myth as History
In some parts of Africa, myths about serpents devouring entire villages or forging hidden underground kingdoms may blend with real events—such as natural disasters, clan migrations, or conflicts over scarce resources. The serpent or "dragon" becomes a symbolic representation of destructive forces. Conversely, a benevolent serpent might recall a leader who saved a people from famine or guided them to fertile land.

---

## 9. Connections to Broader Dragon Archetypes

### 9.1 Shared Motifs with Other Regions
When comparing Sub-Saharan African serpent myths to the dragon stories of Asia, Europe, or the Americas, we see overlapping motifs: guardians of water, keepers of treasure, shape-shifting powers, and cosmic or moral authority. These parallels suggest that certain themes—such as the link between serpents and rainfall—are nearly universal, rooted in the fundamental human need to explain and control natural forces.

### 9.2 Local Interpretations of Foreign Dragons
As African societies encountered European colonizers or Arab merchants who spoke of dragons in their own lore, they sometimes merged these accounts with existing serpent traditions. However, the local emphasis typically remained on water, fertility, and social harmony. The Western image of a winged, fire-breathing monster did not usually displace the older African notion of serpents, though it might appear in some modern syncretic tales (beyond our current historical scope).

### 9.3 Symbolic vs. Literal Belief
It can be tricky to discern how literally past communities believed in giant serpents. In many African cultures, the line between symbolic myth and lived reality is fluid. A serpent might be both a real animal and a channel for spiritual power. This dual perception keeps the serpent's (or dragon's) mythic significance alive in ritual, communal memory, and moral discourse.

# CHAPTER EIGHT: DRAGONS OF THE AMERICAS (PRE-COLUMBIAN MYTHS)

## Introduction

Long before the arrival of Europeans, the Americas were home to great civilizations with rich mythological systems. Across Mesoamerica, the Andes, and North America, people told stories of cosmic serpents, feathered dragons, and other reptilian beings that governed natural forces or connected realms of existence. While Western-style dragons—winged, fire-breathing beasts—are not common in pre-Columbian myths, the notion of a powerful serpent-creature with divine or semi-divine attributes appears frequently.

In this chapter, we will explore key dragon-like figures from the pre-Columbian Americas. We begin with Mesoamerica, where the Feathered Serpent, called Quetzalcoatl among the Aztecs and Kukulkan among the Maya, stands out as a major deity linked to creation, fertility, and kingship. Then we move to South America, focusing on Andean myths of giant serpents like the Amaru, associated with water and the underworld. We will also briefly survey North American indigenous tales of horned serpents, water monsters, and serpent-guardians of sacred sites. By examining these traditions, we see that reptilian archetypes—whether feathered, horned, or cosmic—held a central place in the spiritual lives of the peoples of the pre-contact Americas.

---

## 1. Defining Dragon-Like Beings in the Pre-Columbian Context

### 1.1 Feathered Serpents vs. Fire-Breathing Dragons
Unlike in Eurasia, where the term "dragon" often conjures images of scales, wings, and fiery breath, many American myths describe serpents that fly through magical or divine means—often by having feathers instead of typical wings. The ability to traverse sky, earth, and underworld realms positions these serpents as mediators of cosmic forces.

### 1.2 Horned and Water-Linked Serpents
In North America, some tribes speak of horned serpents that dwell in lakes or rivers, controlling storms or healing powers. This motif is reminiscent of dragons

in other cultures, as it involves a powerful reptile associated with water. Similar ideas appear in South America, where serpents may combine fish-like or avian features, blending categories of the natural world into a single supernatural entity.

### 1.3 Connections to Agriculture and Kingship
In many of these myths, the serpent or dragon-like being is not a malevolent monster but rather a key figure in the cycle of fertility, rain, and agriculture. Kings and priests might claim ancestry from such a being, reinforcing their right to rule and their duty to maintain cosmic balance. This echoes traditions in Africa and Asia, where serpentine creatures legitimize leadership and connect rulers to the divine.

---

## 2. Mesoamerica: Quetzalcoatl, Kukulkan, and the Feathered Serpent Traditions

### 2.1 The Olmec and Early Serpent Imagery
Though best known from Aztec and Maya cultures, the concept of a feathered serpent may date back to the Olmec civilization (1500–400 BCE) along the Gulf Coast of Mexico. Olmec art includes depictions of supernatural creatures merging feline, reptilian, and avian traits. Some scholars interpret these images as precursors to the later Feathered Serpent deity. Though the evidence is fragmentary, it suggests that serpent worship in Mesoamerica has very ancient roots.

### 2.2 Teotihuacan and the Feathered Serpent
The city of Teotihuacan (c. 100 BCE–550 CE), located near modern Mexico City, was a major urban center whose influence spread across Mesoamerica. One of its great pyramids is dedicated to the Feathered Serpent, as seen in sculptures along the temple façade. These portray a plumed serpent head paired with a headdress-like collar, repeating along the pyramid's sides.

While the exact name of the deity at Teotihuacan is unknown (the term "Quetzalcoatl" is Aztec), the symbolism indicates a powerful entity associated with rain, fertility, and warfare. The repeated motif of shells alongside the serpent heads suggests links to water and cosmic life force. When Teotihuacan declined, this Feathered Serpent cult likely spread to other regions, shaping local variations.

## 2.3 The Aztec Quetzalcoatl

The Aztecs, who rose to power in central Mexico in the 14th and 15th centuries, revered Quetzalcoatl as one of their principal gods. His name combines "quetzal" (a brightly colored bird) and "coatl" (snake), literally "Feathered Serpent." Aztec myths depict Quetzalcoatl as a creator deity involved in shaping humanity and bestowing agriculture. He was also associated with the wind, often wearing the Ehecatl mask.

Quetzalcoatl's role went beyond creation. He embodied learning, priesthood, and moral virtue. Some stories portray him as an exiled god who would one day return, linking him with prophecies of cosmic renewal. In certain myths, he opposes Tezcatlipoca (a more warlike and trickster deity), highlighting a moral tension within the Aztec pantheon. Though Quetzalcoatl is no typical "dragon," he fulfills many dragon-like roles: bridging the sky and earth, wielding immense power, and serving as a mediator between gods and humans.

## 2.4 The Maya Kukulkan

Among the Maya, especially in the Postclassic period (c. 900–1500 CE), the Feathered Serpent deity is known as Kukulkan (in Yucatec Maya) or Gucumatz (in K'iche'). Like Quetzalcoatl, Kukulkan is linked to creation, kingship, and the forces of rain and wind. Major Maya centers such as Chichen Itza feature impressive architecture devoted to Kukulkan, including the famous El Castillo pyramid, where a serpent-shaped shadow descends during the equinox—a striking blend of astronomical knowledge and mythic imagery.

The Maya viewed Kukulkan as a bringer of civilization, teaching people agriculture, writing, and the arts. Priests and rulers claimed Kukulkan's favor or lineage, ensuring both cosmic and social order. Rituals dedicated to Kukulkan often aimed to secure rainfall and abundant harvests. The combination of serpent (the earth or underworld) and feathers (the sky) symbolizes the deity's encompassing power over multiple realms.

## 2.5 Local Variations in Mesoamerica

Beyond the major Aztec and Maya polities, numerous smaller groups had their own serpent deities, some strongly resembling Quetzalcoatl or Kukulkan, others with distinct local names and traits. In many areas, the serpent figure was intimately tied to water sources, echoes of which we see in the design of city-states that featured cenotes (natural sinkholes) or rivers considered sacred.

All these traditions highlight how deeply the feathered serpent idea influenced Mesoamerican culture for over a millennium before European contact.

---

## 3. South America: The Andean Amaru and Related Serpent Myths

### 3.1 The Andean Cosmos
The Andes region, encompassing modern-day Peru, Bolivia, Ecuador, and parts of Colombia and Chile, produced civilizations like the Chavín, Moche, Nazca, Wari, and the Inca. These cultures had complex cosmologies that linked the sky (hanan pacha), the earth (kay pacha), and the underworld (uku pacha). Serpent-like beings often served as bridges between these realms.

### 3.2 The Amaru
In Inca and pre-Inca traditions, the Amaru (also spelled Amarú) is a giant serpent sometimes described with multiple heads or a mix of bird and feline features. It dwells underground or in lakes, emerging to connect the underworld and surface. Some Andean imagery shows a two-headed serpent, possibly representing duality—life and death, sky and earth, male and female. The Amaru was not always benevolent; in some myths, it represented earthquakes or floods. In others, it carried messages between gods and mortals.

### 3.3 Chavín and Moche Serpent Imagery
The Chavín culture (c. 900–200 BCE) left behind stone carvings depicting fanged deities with serpent hair or serpent belts, reminiscent of the Olmec approach to combining animal features. Meanwhile, the Moche (c. 100–700 CE) produced stunning ceramics that include serpent-like creatures with stylized heads. Scholars debate whether these represent distinct dragon deities or symbolic references to water, fertility, and transformation. Regardless, the recurring serpent motif underlines the reptile's importance in Andean spirituality.

### 3.4 Inca Beliefs and Rituals
Inca state religion often emphasized the worship of Inti (the Sun) and Viracocha (a creator deity). However, serpents appeared in myths about Viracocha's actions, particularly regarding the creation of lakes or the rearrangement of landscapes. The Inca capital, Cusco, was sometimes said to be designed in the shape of a puma, but serpents also appeared on temple carvings and in the knotted patterns of quipu (record-keeping devices). While not always the central

figure in Inca cosmology, the serpent's presence as a potent symbol of the underworld and life-giving waters remains clear.

---

## 4. North America: Horned Serpents, Underwater Panthers, and Guardian Dragons

### 4.1 The Horned Serpent Motif (Eastern Woodlands)
Many indigenous tribes of North America's Eastern Woodlands—such as the Iroquois, Cherokee, and Muscogee—have stories of a horned serpent dwelling in lakes or rivers. The Cherokee call this being the Uktena, describing it as a massive snake with antlers or a gem in its forehead. It can bestow power or healing on those who approach it correctly, but it can also be deadly, breathing poison or striking with lightning.

This horned serpent often appears as the counterpart to the Thunderbird, a sky spirit that wages constant battle with underworld serpents. Similar to dragons in other cultures, the serpent manages water and rainfall, while the Thunderbird represents celestial forces. Their conflict reflects the balance between sky and earth, a theme repeated in numerous indigenous mythic traditions.

### 4.2 The Great Serpent Mound
In modern-day Ohio, a famous prehistoric earthwork known as the Great Serpent Mound attests to ancient reverence for serpentine imagery. Built by the Adena or Fort Ancient cultures (c. 1000 BCE–AD 1200), the mound depicts a large coiled serpent. Although direct textual evidence is lacking, many archaeologists believe it held religious or ceremonial significance, possibly relating to astronomy. The design suggests that serpents played a role in the region's cosmology, echoing the widespread association between snakes, fertility, and cyclical renewal.

### 4.3 Underwater Panther and Other Water Beasts
Among some Algonquian-speaking tribes, the water-dwelling monster can take the form of a hybrid cat-serpent known as the Mishipeshu or Underwater Panther. While not purely a "dragon," this creature has scales, horns, or spines and inhabits lakes, controlling storms and water traffic. Rivalry between the Underwater Panther and the Thunderbird is a central motif, symbolizing the

clash of underworld and sky powers. Stories describe how disrespecting the lake or failing to honor the creature can lead to drowning or violent storms.

### 4.4 Guardian Serpents of the Southwest
In the deserts of the American Southwest, Puebloan peoples speak of serpentine beings that guard springs or kivas (ceremonial chambers). Although these stories are often not as elaborate as the Mesoamerican myths, they reflect a consistent idea: serpentine spirits maintain vital water sources, bridging the physical and spiritual realms. Heroes or shamans might venture to negotiate with these guardians, ensuring the community's survival in harsh climates.

---

## 5. Dragon-Like Themes and Symbolism in the Pre-Columbian Americas

### 5.1 The Snake-Bird Union
A recurring theme in Mesoamerican, Andean, and some North American myths is the merging of snake and bird characteristics. Birds represent the sky, often linked to wind, rain, or even the sun. Snakes represent earth, water, and the underworld. Combining them yields a being that spans multiple cosmic layers—a key function of dragons in many global traditions.

### 5.2 Mediators Between Realms
In nearly all these myths, the serpent or dragon-like figure connects worlds: the human realm with the supernatural, the mortal with the divine, and the physical with the spiritual. Whether the being is Quetzalcoatl teaching agriculture or a horned serpent offering shamanic visions, it stands as a threshold guardian or guide. This role parallels the draconic function in Asia and elsewhere, where dragons often mediate between gods and mortals.

### 5.3 Legitimizing Power and Social Order
Leaders in Mesoamerica and the Andes frequently claimed descent from or favor with serpent deities. Public rituals, monumental art, and temple complexes dedicated to these beings reinforced a ruler's position. Control over rainfall, harvest, and cosmic balance was essential to maintaining social harmony in agrarian societies—hence the serpent's link to political and religious authority.

## 5.4 Cyclical Regeneration and Time
Many American indigenous calendars and myth cycles revolve around themes of death, rebirth, and cyclical time. The serpent, which sheds its skin, naturally symbolizes renewal. In Mesoamerica, the Feathered Serpent's cyclical reappearance or predicted return tied into larger beliefs about ages of the world. Similarly, Andean myths involving serpents may stress the cyclical rhythms of agriculture and seasonal change.

---

# 6. Archaeological Traces of Serpent Worship

## 6.1 Pyramid and Temple Architecture
From the Pyramid of the Feathered Serpent at Teotihuacan to the Castillo at Chichen Itza, monumental sites in Mesoamerica reflect the importance of serpent deities. Sculptural details—such as serpent heads projecting from temple facades—indicate elaborate rituals. Archaeologists have uncovered offerings like shells, obsidian blades, and figurines placed inside or beneath these structures, demonstrating the depth of devotion to these gods.

## 6.2 Ceramics, Textiles, and Metalwork
In the Andean region, Moche pottery often shows images of fanged serpents or composite monsters. Later Inca metalwork features stylized serpents used in religious or ceremonial contexts. North American rock art at various sites includes horned serpents, providing clues to local worship practices. Taken together, these artifacts affirm that serpent reverence was widespread and integral to Pre-Columbian spiritual life.

## 6.3 Ritual Offerings and Sacrifices
Certain Mesoamerican rituals involved the sacrifice of animals (and sometimes humans) to appease or honor serpent deities. At Templo Mayor in Tenochtitlan, archaeologists found offerings that included serpent carvings dedicated to Huitzilopochtli and Tlaloc—two major Aztec gods who sometimes overlapped with Quetzalcoatl's sphere of influence. While modern sensibilities may find these rites harsh, they were part of the sacred economy that kept cosmic order in balance, often linking serpent imagery with the life-death cycle.

# 7. Oral Traditions and Ancestral Memories

### 7.1 Preservation Through Storytelling
Even after the collapse of major civilizations like the Maya or the Aztec empire, local communities continued to pass down serpent myths orally. In remote villages, the feathered serpent might transform into a local spirit that resides in a nearby cave or mountain. Similarly, Andean highland communities preserved memories of the Amaru or other serpent beings through festival dances, storytelling, and weaving motifs.

### 7.2 Variation Across Regions
Given the wide geographic range of the Americas, serpent myths exhibit enormous diversity. The same root concept—an otherworldly snake that wields elemental power—can look very different in the Amazon, the Great Plains, or the Arctic. Some stories depict the serpent as benevolent, others as menacing. Yet the core imagery of a reptile transcending normal boundaries remains strikingly consistent.

---

# 8. Historical Shifts and Cultural Blending

### 8.1 Influence of Trade and Conquest
In Mesoamerica, powerful states like Teotihuacan, the Toltecs, and eventually the Aztecs spread serpent worship across wide areas through trade and military expansion. Artistic styles—such as the feathered serpent design—traveled with merchants and warriors, often merging with local interpretations. Thus, a common visual language of serpent-deities emerged among distant city-states.

### 8.2 The Southern Connection
Some scholars suggest that the concept of a winged or feathered serpent traveled beyond Mesoamerica into northern parts of South America via trade routes along Central America's isthmus. Although evidence is scarce, certain iconographic parallels—feathered reptiles on pottery or stelae—hint at cross-cultural influence. Over centuries, these exchanges blended with indigenous beliefs, producing localized serpent forms that might be part-bird, part-jaguar, part-snake.

### 8.3 Resilience in the Face of Change

Even as new empires arose—like the Inca in South America or the Mississippian cultures in North America—serpent imagery retained significance. The Mississippian societies built mound complexes and used serpent motifs on ceremonial objects, possibly influenced by earlier cultures like the Hopewell or Adena. Each generation adapted existing serpent symbols to fit new social and religious frameworks, preserving continuity amid rapid change.

---

## 9. Comparing American Dragon-Like Beings to Old World Dragons

### 9.1 Similarities

- **Control of Weather and Fertility**: As with African and Asian dragons, many American serpent deities command rain, storms, or rivers, vital for agriculture.
- **Mediation of Realms**: Like the Chinese dragon bridging Heaven and Earth, feathered serpents or horned serpents connect sky, land, and underworld.
- **Association with Royalty**: Rulers use serpent imagery to legitimize power, mirroring the imperial dragons of China or serpent-based claims of African kingships.

### 9.2 Differences

- **Feathers Instead of Wings**: The most iconic difference is the frequent depiction of serpents with plumage rather than bat-like wings.
- **Moral Alignment**: While many European tales frame dragons as evil, Mesoamerican and Andean serpents often play positive or ambivalent roles, guiding civilization rather than threatening it.
- **Less Emphasis on Hoarding Treasure**: Although some serpents guard resources (water, sacred items), the notion of a dragon's lair filled with gold is less prominent in pre-Columbian lore.

---

# CHAPTER NINE: MEDIEVAL EUROPEAN DRAGONS AND LEGENDS

## Introduction

By the medieval period, the lands once controlled by the Roman Empire had shifted into many small kingdoms, duchies, and principalities. The Christian Church gained significant power, Germanic and other "barbarian" groups had reshaped local cultures, and a new age of chivalry and feudalism was emerging. Throughout these changes, the dragon concept remained important in folk stories, literature, and art. However, the shape and symbolism of dragons in medieval Europe differed from what we have seen in earlier eras.

This chapter explores how dragons appeared in medieval European culture. We will look at local legends of dragons terrorizing the countryside, the role of dragons in courtly romances and epic poetry, the influence of bestiaries on how people viewed these creatures, and how knights, warriors, or saints might confront them in popular tales. We also examine the ways these stories reflected social values, religious beliefs, and Europe's patchwork of cultural influences. By the end, we will see that the medieval dragon became a powerful emblem of both fear and moral testing, often intertwined with Christian themes that shaped its identity.

---

## 1. The Shifting World of Early Medieval Europe

### 1.1 End of the Western Roman Empire
After the collapse of the Western Roman Empire in the 5th century, Europe fragmented into successor states ruled by various tribes: Goths, Vandals, Lombards, Franks, and others. While some Roman traditions survived, new rulers brought their own myths and beliefs. In previous chapters, we noted how Germanic peoples had wyrm stories, and Celtic groups had legends of serpentine monsters. These cultural threads wove together under a broadening Christian framework, gradually producing what we now call "medieval Europe."

### 1.2 Local Traditions and Christian Influence
As Christianity spread, many older beliefs about serpents and monstrous foes

were reinterpreted. Rather than discarding them, medieval storytellers often recast them in a Christian moral framework. Dragons could be described as diabolical forces, monstrous representations of sin, or trials sent by God to test the faithful. But in the daily life of small communities, the dragon also continued as a figure in folklore—an unknown creature lurking beyond the village, in caves or remote hillsides.

### 1.3 Cultural Exchange and Hybrid Legends

Trade routes crisscrossed Europe, bringing goods and stories from distant lands. Pilgrimages to holy sites, diplomatic marriages among noble families, and the travels of knights all contributed to the blending of local dragon tales. Over time, certain motifs—like the heroic knight confronting a terrible dragon—became staples of European storytelling, merging Celtic, Germanic, Latin, and Christian influences into a distinct medieval pattern.

---

## 2. Dragons in Medieval Bestiaries and Scholarly Works

### 2.1 The Purpose of Bestiaries

Bestiaries were collections of descriptions about real and mythical animals, compiled by medieval monks or scholars who sought to catalog the wonders of God's creation. They drew on earlier sources, such as Pliny the Elder's *Natural History* and Greek or Roman accounts, but also included Christian allegories. Dragons appeared in nearly every bestiary, typically presented as the largest or most fearsome of serpents.

### 2.2 Descriptions and Symbolism

Bestiaries often emphasized the dragon's snake-like body, wings (in many cases), sharp claws, and occasionally the ability to breathe fire or emit poison. These texts sometimes cited "observations" of dragons in distant lands—like India or Ethiopia—echoing older classical ideas. Yet the moral lesson was central: the dragon usually symbolized the devil or the embodiment of pride, warning the reader that evil can appear powerful, but righteous faith or virtue can ultimately overcome it.

### 2.3 Influence on Art and Imagination

Medieval artists used bestiaries as references for manuscript illuminations, church carvings, and stained-glass windows. A dragon might appear coiled around pillars, menacing biblical figures or saints, or placed in corners of a church doorway to represent lurking sin. These images shaped popular thinking: even illiterate peasants could see stone carvings of dragons on a cathedral and absorb the notion that dragons were terrifying foes, yet conquerable by divine or saintly power.

---

## 3. Local Legends: Dragons as Rural Menaces

### 3.1 Folk Tales and Oral Tradition
In many parts of Europe, stories circulated of dragons in remote caves or marshes that terrorized entire communities. These dragons demanded tribute—sometimes livestock, sometimes a maiden as a sacrifice—and local folk might recount how a brave man (perhaps a knight or a peasant with cunning) slew the beast. While such tales share similarities with older Greek or Roman myths (like Perseus and Andromeda), the medieval versions often emphasize Christian faith, moral purity, or the gallantry of knighthood.

### 3.2 Examples from Britain, France, and Germany

- **Britain**: Tales of the "Lambton Worm" or "Laidly Worm" revolve around monstrous serpents ravaging the countryside. Often, the hero belongs to a local noble family, and the story ends with the creature's defeat, saving the community.
- **France**: Legends such as the "Tarasque" in Provence describe a dragon-like monster with a spiked shell, terrorizing villages until a saint or hero pacifies it.
- **Germany**: In regions along the Rhine, there are narratives of lurking Lindwurms or draconic beasts in thick forests, often requiring a knight or cunning youth to dispatch them, sometimes with the help of magic or holy relics.

Though each region has unique local names and features, the pattern remains: a monstrous reptile menaces the land, and it falls to a bold champion (often with moral or divine backing) to fight and restore peace.

### 3.3 Social and Cultural Meanings
Such folk tales reflect communal fears: the unknown wilderness, devastating raids, disease, or famine. By personifying these threats as a dragon, storytellers

gave shape to anxieties. The hero's triumph symbolized the reestablishment of order and safety—an affirmation that with courage, faith, and sometimes cunning, communities could endure hardships. Meanwhile, the maiden sacrifice trope underscored the idea of innocence imperiled by evil. By preventing her death, the hero upheld societal values of purity and protection of the vulnerable.

---

## 4. The Knight and the Dragon: Courtly Romances and Epic Poetry

### 4.1 Chivalry and the Dragon
The medieval ideal of chivalry stressed bravery, honor, loyalty to one's lord, and protection of the weak. Dragons featured in many chivalric romances precisely because they presented the ultimate challenge. Slaying (or defeating) a dragon tested a knight's valor and proved his worth as a defender of the realm. In some stories, the act of conquering a dragon also indicated divine favor, as it suggested the knight was an instrument of God's justice.

### 4.2 Famous Literary Examples

- **"Bevis of Hampton"**: An English romance where the hero performs many feats, including fighting dragons, showcasing both martial prowess and piety.
- **"Guy of Warwick"**: Another popular English tale in which the titular knight battles giants, monsters, and occasionally dragons to win favor and prove devotion to his lady.
- **French Romances**: While not as frequent as in English lore, French knightly tales sometimes feature serpent-like beasts or references to older stories. The hero's confrontation with a dragon demonstrates knightly virtue and cements his reputation.

In these narratives, the dragon rarely receives deep characterization; it is primarily an obstacle or symbol of ultimate danger. The focus lies on the knight's moral and physical qualities.

### 4.3 Arthurian Legends
Although the core Arthurian cycle (as popularized by Chrétien de Troyes, Thomas Malory, and others) does not revolve heavily around dragons, the motif does appear. Knights of the Round Table undertake quests involving monstrous creatures, occasionally including draconic foes. More broadly, the dragon shape

is used in heraldic devices (a topic covered later in the book), tying the creature to royal or knightly identities.

### 4.4 Literary Impact and Spread of Themes

These dragon-slaying adventures traveled across Europe through translated manuscripts, troubadour songs, and traveling minstrels. They resonated with feudal society's emphasis on martial skill and moral righteousness. As a result, the image of the knight vs. dragon became almost synonymous with medieval heroism—an iconic duel repeated in countless variations, influencing art, drama, and local storytelling traditions.

---

## 5. Dragons Beyond the Knightly Quest: The "Wyrm" Continuation

### 5.1 Legacy of Germanic and Norse Wyrms

We have already explored how Northern Europe's early medieval cultures told of wyrms or serpents, such as the one in *Beowulf*. In later medieval centuries, these wyrms continued as part of local lore. They could be wingless dragons or giant snakes, sometimes with partial limbs. They haunted bogs or barrows, guarding treasure or dooming anyone who ventured near.

### 5.2 Blurring of Categories

By the High Middle Ages (roughly 11th to 13th centuries), distinctions between wingless wyrms, lindwurms, and classic dragons with wings and fiery breath could become blurred. Some texts used the term "dragon" broadly to describe any large serpentine monster. Others preserved older local terms like *ormr* or *worm*. Regardless, the general concept of a dangerous reptilian beast remained, adapted to local landscapes and narrative needs.

### 5.3 Moral and Cultural Functions

Wyrms in these stories served as cautionary tales about greed (treasure-guarding monsters), or as signs of ancestral curses if an unscrupulous act had been committed. They could also appear in parables about pride or sin. The monstrous wyrm, easy to demonize, allowed storytellers to impart lessons about moral behavior, reinforcing communal ethics under a Christian worldview.

---

# 6. Dragons and Medieval Pseudoscience: "Real" Accounts

### 6.1 Travelers' Tales and Wonders of the East
Medieval Europe produced many travelogues or compendia describing strange creatures in distant lands, often building on older Greek or Roman misconceptions. Writers like Sir John Mandeville (in a 14th-century text, whose authorship remains uncertain) claimed to have encountered serpents so large they swallowed elephants, echoing classical claims from Pliny. These descriptions fueled the belief that dragons were real but lived far beyond Europe's borders—perhaps in Africa, the Middle East, or Asia.

### 6.2 "Eyewitness" Claims
Occasionally, local chronicles in Europe mention sightings of dragons, typically framed as omens. A monk might record that a dragon was seen flying over a town's rooftops or across a battlefield. Such reports could be exaggerations, misidentified natural phenomena, or symbolic metaphors. Still, they reveal that many people in the Middle Ages did not view dragons as purely fictional. Instead, dragons occupied a hazy zone between myth and potential reality.

### 6.3 Impact on Herbalism and Medicine
Some medieval herbals or medical texts reference dragon parts—teeth, blood, or organs—said to have miraculous properties. Though these items were likely derived from crocodiles or large snakes, the label "dragon" gave them an exotic allure. Apocryphal remedies included "dragon's blood" (actually a type of resin) believed to cure ailments or protect against evil. Such beliefs blended superstition, limited scientific knowledge, and the strong symbolic pull of the dragon's name.

---

# 7. The Dragon as Diabolical Force

### 7.1 Church Doctrine and Sin Symbolism
While Chapter Ten focuses in depth on early Christian writings about dragons, it is worth noting here that by the medieval era, the Church's teaching often equated dragons with demons or the devil. Sermons, religious plays, and moral tracts depicted dragons as outward images of inner vice. Priests might compare the seven heads of a dragon to the Seven Deadly Sins, warning that to allow one's soul to be dominated by greed, pride, or lust would invite a dragon-like corruption.

## 7.2 Cathedral Imagery and Gargoyles
Gargoyles carved in the shape of dragons, chimeras, or serpentine beasts adorned many cathedrals. Partly functional as water spouts, they also served a symbolic purpose: these monstrous faces reminded viewers of the evils lurking outside God's grace. Their presence on the holy building's exterior underscored the idea that the church protected the faithful from demonic influences. The imagery of monstrous reptiles thus reinforced Christian cosmology, placing dragons among the devils repelled by sanctity.

## 7.3 Miracle Plays and Dramatizations
Medieval religious plays, especially in parts of England and France, sometimes dramatized events where a saint or angel fought a dragon, representing triumph over evil. While these performances were rooted in biblical or saintly lore, the spectacle of a dragon being vanquished on stage gave commoners a vivid demonstration of Christian victory over sin. Even if the dragon was a simple puppet or costume, the storyline resonated with medieval moral teachings.

---

# 8. Dragon Encounters in Chronicles and Legend Collections

## 8.1 Medieval Chroniclers
Writers like Geoffrey of Monmouth, William of Malmesbury, or Saxo Grammaticus preserved stories of wondrous beasts in their historical or pseudo-historical works. Dragons sometimes featured as portents of dynastic changes or catastrophes. A local account might say that a dragon was seen in the sky, predicting a king's downfall. Although modern scholars classify such tales as myth or propaganda, medieval readers often accepted them as factual or at least plausible.

## 8.2 Collections of Wonders and Miracles
Beyond formal chronicles, medieval scribes compiled anthologies of miracles and marvels, some of which included dragon episodes. A region might claim a relic from a dragon-slaying event—a scale or bone displayed in a church as proof of a saint's deed. Pilgrims traveling to see these relics would carry the story onward. In this way, local legends about dragons entered broader European awareness.

## 8.3 Knights' Tales in Popular Culture
Late medieval romances, ballads, and poems continued to feature dragons as

tests for knights. Minstrels performed stories in castle halls or at village fairs, ensuring that even those who could not read encountered the dragon motif. These performances made the dragon a shared cultural icon: when people heard the word "dragon," they imagined a towering, fire-spewing beast that challenged the bravest of heroes and, by extension, human virtue itself.

## 9. Dragons and Medieval Urban Legends

### 9.1 The Dragon in the City
While many dragon tales focus on rural or wilderness settings, some medieval stories place dragons in urban contexts—dwelling under bridges, in city sewers, or abandoned wells. Such accounts often sprang from real problems like disease or strange noises in subterranean tunnels. People struggling to explain the unknown might attribute it to a dragon lurking below the city. Enterprising knights or civic leaders might vow to eliminate this hidden threat, whether real or imagined.

### 9.2 Civic Identity and Dragon Lore
Cities sometimes adopted a dragon motif in their coats of arms or civic legends. For instance, a city might claim an ancient hero drove a dragon from the region, symbolizing the founding moment. Though these legends may have little historical basis, they infused communal pride and gave the populace a mythic anchor for local identity.

### 9.3 Taming the Dragon
Occasionally, the story ends not with the dragon's death, but with its taming. A saint or holy figure might bind the dragon, leading it through town as proof of divine authority. This is similar to the Tarasque legend in France, where the monstrous creature is subdued by a saint's prayer rather than a knight's sword. Such "tamed dragon" tales highlight another dimension: the power of mercy, humility, or sanctity to overcome monstrous evil.

## 10. Varied Dragon Forms in Medieval Europe

### 10.1 Multiple Heads, Poisonous Breath, and Fire
The standard medieval dragon often combined serpent-like features with bat-like wings, clawed legs, and a mouth breathing fire or poisonous fumes. However, the number of heads varied in local stories. Some dragons had more than one head, echoing older myths like the Lernaean Hydra. Medieval illustrators also loved to depict bright scales, spiked tails, and glowing eyes, emphasizing the dragon's supernatural terror.

### 10.2 The Wyvern
A wyvern is a specific heraldic form of dragon with two legs (instead of four) and wings. In medieval lore, it might appear as a lesser form of dragon or a regional variant. Some bestiaries called it a "serpent with wings," distinguishing it from the "true" four-legged dragon, but popular usage often blurred the lines. Wyverns still carried strong negative connotations, representing pestilence or war in certain coats of arms.

### 10.3 Sea Dragons and Draconic Hybrids
In coastal regions, there were stories of sea dragons or sea serpents, monstrous creatures that menaced ships. Medieval maps sometimes labeled uncharted waters with phrases like "Here be dragons." While these references do not prove actual sightings, they reflect deep-seated anxieties about the unknown ocean depths. Hybrids—like half-fish, half-reptile dragons—entered medieval bestiaries, bridging the gap between land beasts and marine terrors.

---

## 11. The Dragon's Role in Moral Allegory

### 11.1 Representation of the Seven Deadly Sins
Medieval preachers sometimes used the dragon as a composite symbol of the vices plaguing human souls. Each head of a multi-headed dragon could stand for a specific sin: pride, greed, lust, envy, gluttony, wrath, and sloth. Confronting the dragon signified moral striving, with the hero or saint slaying each sin, one by one.

### 11.2 Triumph of Good over Evil
In general Christian allegory, the dragon signified evil, chaos, and temptation. Its

defeat by a righteous person—whether a biblical figure, saint, or knight—demonstrated that faith and virtue could prevail. Sermons and religious art hammered home this lesson: no matter how terrifying the dragon appears, it cannot withstand the light of truth and the sword of righteousness.

### 11.3 Complexities of Medieval Thought

Despite the dragon's overall negative portrayal, medieval authors sometimes recognized that the dragon was also part of God's creation. Bestiaries might claim it had a place in the natural order, albeit as a fearsome predator or a test for humanity. This dual perspective—both condemning the dragon as evil and acknowledging it as a creature under divine authority—reflects the complexity of medieval theology, where everything served a higher plan, even monstrous beasts.

# CHAPTER TEN: DRAGONS IN EARLY CHRISTIAN WRITINGS

## Introduction

Christianity, from its earliest days, grappled with the idea of serpents and dragons. The religion emerged in a world already rich with Jewish, Greek, and Roman lore about monstrous reptiles, and as it spread, it encountered a variety of local serpent myths. Early Christian authors, apologists, and theologians reinterpreted these traditions in light of the new faith's teachings. In time, the dragon became a central image representing the forces of evil, with references drawn from both Hebrew scriptures and new Christian visions, especially in the Book of Revelation.

This chapter explores how dragons appear in the earliest Christian writings, from the New Testament era through the works of the early Church Fathers and into the formative centuries of Christendom. We look at how biblical texts shaped Christian interpretations of dragons, how Church leaders used the dragon image to teach moral lessons, and how saintly legends involving dragons—often based on older pagan motifs—were transformed into vehicles of Christian doctrine. Ultimately, we see that the Christian view of the dragon as a symbol of the devil or sin had a profound influence on medieval and later European culture.

---

## 1. Biblical Foundations

### 1.1 Old Testament Serpents and Leviathan
Though the Hebrew Bible does not typically use the word "dragon" as modern readers imagine it, it contains references to sea monsters and serpents such as Leviathan (in Job, Psalms, and Isaiah) and Rahab (in Isaiah). These creatures sometimes appear as symbols of chaos, cosmic adversaries that God subdues. By the time of early Christianity, Greek translations of Hebrew texts (such as the Septuagint) rendered some of these terms as "drakon," contributing to the link between biblical serpents and dragons.

### 1.2 The Serpent in Eden
The Book of Genesis describes the serpent that tempts Adam and Eve, leading to

the Fall. While the text does not call this creature a "dragon," later Christian tradition increasingly viewed it as the devil or Satan in reptilian form. By extension, some early Christian writers merged the serpent of Eden with broader imagery of a dragon, describing this being as one who had once been an angel but now prowled the world, seeking to corrupt humankind.

### 1.3 New Testament Passages
The New Testament itself rarely mentions serpents in a draconic sense, except for the Book of Revelation (discussed below). Nonetheless, Jesus' statement to be "wise as serpents" (Matthew 10:16) and references to serpents as dangerous (Luke 10:19) contributed to the broader Christian view that serpents signified caution, danger, or evil—though sometimes cunning or intelligence as well.

---

## 2. The Book of Revelation: The Great Red Dragon

### 2.1 Apocalyptic Imagery
The Book of Revelation (also called the Apocalypse of John) was likely written in the late 1st century AD. It contains vivid visions of cosmic battles and the end of the present world order. Central to its symbolism is "the great red dragon," which attempts to devour a child destined to rule nations (Revelation 12). Later, this dragon is explicitly identified with "that ancient serpent, who is called the devil and Satan" (Revelation 12:9; 20:2).

### 2.2 The Dragon's Role in the Cosmic Conflict
In Revelation, the dragon leads a rebellion in heaven, fights against the archangel Michael, and is cast down to earth. This narrative fuses older Judaic concepts of cosmic chaos monsters with Christian teaching that Satan is the ultimate adversary of God's kingdom. By calling him both "dragon" and "ancient serpent," the text unites the Edenic tempter with the monstrous figure of a cosmic beast. Early Christians thus had a clear scriptural basis to see the dragon as the devil incarnate.

### 2.3 Lasting Influence
Revelation's imagery profoundly shaped Christian art, preaching, and theology for centuries. As the religion spread, the idea that dragons were diabolical agents of Satan became a cornerstone of Christian belief. This view influenced how the faithful perceived real reptiles (like snakes and crocodiles) and how they interpreted local serpent-lore, as well as how they saw monstrous reptiles in legend: these were all illusions or manifestations of demonic power.

## 3. Early Church Fathers and the Dragon Motif

### 3.1 Tertullian and the Serpent
Tertullian (c. 155–220 AD), an influential Christian writer from Carthage, often invoked the serpent of Eden in his arguments against heresy. While he did not devote entire treatises to "dragons," he associated serpentine imagery with deception and the devil's cunning. Drawing on Revelation, Tertullian saw the devil as a reptilian deceiver working through false teachings to lead Christians astray.

### 3.2 Origen's Allegorical Interpretations
Origen of Alexandria (c. 184–253 AD) used allegory extensively to interpret biblical texts. In his commentaries, the dragon of Revelation might represent not just Satan personally but all structures of evil, including persecuting governments or human vices. Origen's approach set a precedent for later theologians: the biblical dragon was real in a spiritual sense—embodying the devil—but also symbolically stood for any force opposing divine truth.

### 3.3 Augustine of Hippo and the Fallen Angel
Saint Augustine (354–430 AD) strongly shaped Western Christian theology. While he did not write a single treatise focusing solely on dragons, he frequently spoke of the devil's serpent-like nature. In works like *The City of God*, Augustine linked pride and rebellion in the angelic ranks to the serpent of Eden and the dragon of Revelation. For Augustine, the devil as dragon represented the most dangerous form of pride, seeking to build an earthly city in opposition to God's heavenly kingdom.

---

## 4. Dragons in Early Christian Apocrypha and Hagiography

### 4.1 Apocryphal Texts
Outside the official biblical canon, numerous apocryphal works circulated among early Christian communities. Some retold Old Testament stories with extra details, occasionally mentioning monstrous reptiles or attributing draconic form to idols destroyed by prophets. While these texts vary in authority and date, they show how Christians continued to blend Jewish, Greek, and Near Eastern dragon imagery into new narratives, typically with an emphasis on proving the supremacy of God over pagan monsters.

## 4.2 Saints and Martyrs Confronting Dragons

Legends of early Christian saints often feature miraculous battles against dragons. Although many of these accounts took shape more fully in the medieval period, some originated in the early centuries. For example:

- **St. Philip**: An apocryphal story has him confront a giant serpent in Hierapolis, though details differ by region.
- **St. Sylvester**: An early 4th-century bishop of Rome, later stories claimed he subdued a dragon-like creature in a cave, demonstrating Christ's power over demonic forces.

These narratives, while sometimes short on historical evidence, served as moral lessons. The saint's victory over the dragon mirrored the triumph of faith over demonic evil.

## 4.3 The Evolution of Saintly Dragon-Slaying

Over time, as these tales spread, they became part of the collective Christian imagination. In many areas, local storytellers attached a "dragon miracle" to a revered bishop or martyr. Though not always grounded in verifiable fact, such legends buttressed the saint's reputation and demonstrated that Christian holiness could literally overcome monstrous adversity.

# 5. Connecting Pagan and Christian Dragon Lore

## 5.1 Assimilation of Pagan Rituals

In the first few centuries after Constantine's conversion (early 4th century AD), the Christian Church gradually absorbed or reinterpreted many pagan practices. Local gods or spirits once depicted as serpents or dragons were recast as demons. Where a region had a serpent cult, Christian missionaries might declare the serpent an evil presence that the local saint or bishop must vanquish. In this way, the older worship was supplanted by a Christian narrative of victory over the devil.

## 5.2 Hybrid Myths and Christianization

In places like Gaul (modern France) or Britain, older Celtic or Germanic dragon legends merged with new Christian messages. The monstrous being might retain a local name or certain folklore traits—like living in a sacred spring or standing guard over the harvest—but now the official story ended with a Christian figure defeating it. The result was a fusion that allowed communities to keep telling old stories, but with a Christian moral that highlighted God's dominance.

### 5.3 Icons and Shrines
Early Christian shrines sometimes featured relief carvings or icons showing saints defeating dragons. While such images became more common in the medieval period, seeds of the tradition were sown early. Pilgrims who visited these shrines would hear stories of how the saint overcame the dragon, reinforcing the link between local identity and Christian triumph. Over generations, these stories crystallized into established legends.

---

## 6. Theological Interpretation of Dragons as Demons

### 6.1 A Consistent Theme
From the earliest writings to the patristic era (2nd–5th centuries AD), Christian thinkers consistently used serpent and dragon imagery to discuss the devil. This made it easy to incorporate local or inherited myths: if a region already had a monstrous serpent tale, the Church could interpret it as a manifestation of Satan's power. Thus, dragons became a universal symbol of evil across culturally diverse Christian communities.

### 6.2 Allegorical Explanations
Church Fathers often explained that the dragon's terrifying features—fire, poison, huge wings, or multiple heads—were metaphors for the many ways the devil attacks believers. Fire could stand for temptation, poison for false doctrine, wings for the devil's ability to appear suddenly or travel swiftly to sow discord. The moral aim was clear: to remind Christians to remain vigilant and steadfast against evil in all its forms.

### 6.3 Casting Out Demons
Early Christian exorcists sometimes described confronting demon-possessed individuals as battling a "dragon" within the afflicted soul. While not literal, this language stressed the seriousness of demonic influence. When exorcisms succeeded, it was akin to a spiritual dragon-slaying—Christ's power forcing the serpent out. Such dramatic imagery resonated with congregations, who already feared dragons from local lore.

---

# 7. Saint George and the Dragon: Early Traces

### 7.1 Origins of the Saint George Legend
One of the most famous dragon-slaying saints is St. George, venerated as a martyr of the early 4th century under Diocletian. While historical facts about George are sparse, devotion to him spread widely in Eastern Christianity first. By the 5th and 6th centuries, churches were dedicated to St. George in the Byzantine Empire, and his cult grew.

### 7.2 Earliest Written Dragon Story
The tale of George fighting a dragon seems to appear in written form somewhat later (likely around the 7th or 8th century in Eastern Christian texts), but many scholars believe it draws on older local myths that were Christianized. The typical story has George rescue a princess and slay a dragon that terrorized a city. The grateful citizens convert to Christianity. While this specific version is more of a medieval romance theme, its seeds lie in the early Christian practice of linking saintly miracles with the defeat of monstrous serpents.

### 7.3 Influence on Later Christian Traditions
As centuries passed, the Saint George legend became one of the primary models for dragon-slaying narratives across Christendom. But the essential link—saintly power defeating a demonic dragon—was already present in earlier Christian lore. By the time we reach the medieval period, this motif had fully blossomed, appearing in countless retellings, icons, and devotionals.

---

# 8. Apocalyptic Dragons and Eschatology in Early Christianity

### 8.1 Heightened Expectation of the End Times
The early Christian community, especially in its first few centuries, lived with a strong sense that Christ's return and the world's end were imminent. Passages about the dragon in Revelation fueled the belief that cosmic battles between good and evil were already underway, culminating in a final showdown where the devil would be bound or destroyed.

### 8.2 Millennial Views
Some groups (often labeled "millenarian" or "chiliast") took Revelation quite literally, expecting a thousand-year reign of Christ after the devil-dragon's defeat. Church authorities often moderated such views, but even more

mainstream writers invoked the image of the dragon's final doom to assure believers that no matter how powerful evil seemed, its time was short. The devil's draconic power, while fearsome, was ultimately inferior to God's.

### 8.3 The Dragon's Place in the Heavenly Drama
Overall, early Christian eschatology placed the dragon at the center of a grand narrative: it was once an angel, rebelled through pride, and became the tempter in Eden, the persecutor of saints, and the final foe to be vanquished. Every mention of a monstrous serpent or dragon in local stories could be woven into this cosmic tapestry, reinforcing the Church's teachings on salvation history.

---

## 9. From Early Writings to Medieval Adoption

### 9.1 Shaping Medieval Perspectives
The ideas formulated in the first several centuries—linking dragons to the devil, highlighting saintly defeats of serpents, and interpreting biblical serpentine imagery—laid the groundwork for how medieval Europeans would view dragons. As Christianity was the central cultural force in medieval Europe, these early Christian concepts fed directly into the bestiaries, moral allegories, and local legends covered in Chapter Nine.

### 9.2 Transition to a Broader Audience
Initially, works by Tertullian, Origen, Augustine, and other Fathers were read by the educated clergy or well-off laity. Over time, as monasticism spread and literacy expanded among monks and nuns, these writings influenced homilies and teachings. The "dragon as devil" theme reached peasants through sermons, church art, and popular retellings, ensuring that even the illiterate masses absorbed the notion of dragons as embodiments of evil.

### 9.3 Cross-Cultural Transmission
Furthermore, Eastern Christian traditions about dragons, especially the cult of saints like George or Theodore, traveled westward through pilgrimages, trade routes, and the exchange of relics. By the early medieval period, the West had adopted these stories, adding its own local flavor and weaving them into the tapestry of European folklore.

# CHAPTER ELEVEN: DRAGON ENCOUNTERS IN THE AGE OF EXPLORATION

## Introduction

The Age of Exploration, roughly spanning the 15th through the early 17th centuries, saw European powers venture beyond their continent in search of new trade routes, wealth, and territories. During this time, explorers, merchants, missionaries, and adventurers traveled to Africa, Asia, and the Americas. Stories of strange beasts came flooding back to Europe. Dragons, long a staple of European folklore, now took on new dimensions as travelers described exotic lands filled with reptiles, serpents, and rumored monsters.

This chapter examines how dragon lore evolved amid the Age of Exploration. We look at how explorers' reports—sometimes firsthand, sometimes exaggerated or entirely fabricated—mixed with existing beliefs. We also consider how contact with foreign cultures, many of which had their own dragon or serpent myths, fueled new tales. In addition, we explore how mapmakers, natural philosophers, and collectors of curiosities handled the idea of dragons in light of the fresh information pouring in from newly encountered regions. While some sought to rationalize or debunk old myths, others clung to or even heightened them, perpetuating the image of dragons as real dangers in distant lands.

---

## 1. Setting the Stage: European Curiosity and Mythic Expectations

### 1.1 Medieval Precedents
Before Columbus's voyages or Vasco da Gama's journey to India, Europeans already had a rich literary background of "wonders of the East." These accounts stemmed from classical writers like Pliny the Elder, medieval bestiaries, and popular travelogues such as the *Travels of Sir John Mandeville*. Many references to serpents or dragons in these works focused on distant lands—India, Ethiopia, or remote Asian regions. So by the dawn of the Age of Exploration, Europeans were primed to believe that dragons or giant serpents might indeed lurk outside their familiar territories.

### 1.2 Religious Motivations
Another factor was religious zeal. Missionaries who ventured abroad hoped to

spread Christianity. Tales of demonic creatures or monstrous reptiles in foreign lands echoed the medieval tradition that dragons were diabolical forces. Some missionaries believed they might literally combat these dragons, much as saints did in older hagiographies. This expectation blended spiritual aims with curiosity, shaping the sort of "dragon stories" they reported.

### 1.3 Royal Patronage and Ambition
Monarchs who sponsored voyages, such as Portugal's Prince Henry the Navigator or Spain's Ferdinand and Isabella, were interested in trade routes and territorial expansion. At the same time, they wanted to dazzle their courts with exotic accounts. Explorers who returned with dramatic tales—whether real or embellished—could gain favor. Thus, sensational stories of monstrous beasts, including dragons, found a receptive audience among royals and nobles, contributing to the mythic aura around uncharted regions.

---

## 2. Encounters (Real and Imagined) in Africa

### 2.1 Coastal Explorations and Reptilian Reports
As Portuguese explorers sailed down the West African coast in the 15th century, they encountered crocodiles, large pythons, and other formidable reptiles. In their writings, these creatures sometimes merged with dragon motifs. A ten-foot python might be described as a fearsome "serpent," reminiscent of the monstrous wyrms back home. Crocodiles, especially if larger than any seen in Europe, were occasionally labeled "dragons" in traveler letters or diaries.

### 2.2 Tales from the Interior
Although European knowledge of Africa's interior remained limited for much of the Age of Exploration, secondhand stories circulated. Local African informants—traders, guides, or coastal intermediaries—spoke of giant snakes in the forests or serpentine water spirits in inland rivers. These beings, which in local contexts might be revered or feared as spiritual guardians, were readily branded "dragons" in European retellings. The concept of a monstrous serpent that controlled water sources or demanded offerings fit neatly into European notions of how dragons behaved.

### 2.3 The "Ethiopian Dragons" Revival
Greek and Roman references to "Ethiopian serpents" or dragons—drawn from classical authors—were revived when explorers encountered the region known

broadly as "Ethiopia" (covering modern Ethiopia and adjacent areas). They looked for confirmation of ancient claims about serpents big enough to fight elephants. While such battles were never witnessed, the rumor mill thrived. Occasional sightings of large pythons or other snakes were seized upon as proof that Ethiopian dragons were real.

## 3. Asia and the Meeting of Dragon Traditions

### 3.1 Arrival in India and Beyond
When Vasco da Gama reached India in 1498, and soon after, Portuguese, Dutch, and other European traders established footholds around the Indian Ocean, they encountered local serpent traditions. India had long myths of the Nagas—powerful serpent beings that could shapeshift. While not precisely "dragons" by European definitions, the Nagas were easily slotted into the same conceptual space. European writers sometimes equated these spiritual serpents with dragons, reporting that India was indeed home to reptilian wonders.

### 3.2 China and the Imperial Dragon
One of the most significant cultural encounters occurred when Europeans began trading with China. The Chinese dragon (*long*), a benevolent symbol of imperial authority, weather, and cosmic harmony, differed sharply from Europe's demonic or monstrous dragon. Early Jesuit missionaries, such as Matteo Ricci (late 16th century), wrote letters describing the Chinese reverence for dragons on flags, architecture, and imperial robes. Back in Europe, these reports caused fascination. Scholars and courtiers realized that not all dragons were feared; in parts of Asia, the creature was revered. This discovery disrupted the purely negative or devilish image of dragons in the European mind and seeded new discussions about cultural relativity.

### 3.3 Encounters in Southeast Asia
In the island regions of Southeast Asia (modern Indonesia, Malaysia, the Philippines), Europeans heard locals speak of *nagas* or serpent-like water deities akin to those in India. Additionally, some explorers saw large monitor lizards or other reptiles unknown in Europe. These sightings, occasionally magnified by rumor, led to stories of dragons inhabiting tropical islands. Though few explorers claimed direct battles with such beasts, the idea of "dragon islands" circulated in seafaring lore, blending Asian serpent-deity concepts with European dragon tradition.

## 4. The New World: Myths in the Americas

### 4.1 Initial Contacts
When Columbus reached the Caribbean in 1492, and later expeditions pushed deeper into the Americas, European adventurers encountered unfamiliar fauna—iguanas, caimans, huge anacondas, and more. Although these creatures were distinct from the legendary dragons of Europe, they sparked curiosity and sometimes fear. Large lizards or crocodilians might be labeled "dragons," especially if accompanied by local stories about serpents or water monsters.

### 4.2 Misunderstandings and Exaggerations
In Mesoamerica and South America, Europeans met civilizations—Aztec, Maya, Inca, among others—with sophisticated myths about feathered serpents (like Quetzalcoatl or Kukulkan) and cosmic snakes (like the Andean Amaru). Conquistadors and chroniclers often conflated these deities with the "dragons" described in medieval bestiaries, concluding that local people worshipped or feared literal dragons. Bernal Díaz del Castillo, a soldier in Cortés's army, wrote of terrifying idols among the Aztecs, which sometimes included serpentine imagery. These misreadings fueled sensational claims that the New World was rife with demon-like dragons.

### 4.3 The Search for Marvels
European courts, hungry for wonders, urged explorers to bring back "dragon relics" or descriptions of monstrous creatures. Some travelers did produce large reptile skins or bones, possibly from anacondas, crocodiles, or extinct creatures. Once displayed in Europe, these finds were often labeled "dragon hides" or "dragon bones," reinforcing the conviction that explorers had indeed found living dragons. In some cases, local American myths about sacred serpents helped shape these interpretations, as the explorers were quick to equate any giant snake or serpent-god with the medieval dragon concept.

---

## 5. Dragon Lore in Maps, Navigation, and Early Science

### 5.1 Cartographic Traditions
Medieval and early Renaissance mapmakers often decorated blank ocean spaces with sea monsters or inscriptions like "Here be dragons." During the Age of Exploration, more detailed charts gradually replaced these older stylized depictions. Yet, in the 15th and 16th centuries, transitional maps still blended

factual coastlines with fanciful beasts. Some depicted dragons near known shipping routes in Asia or Africa, reflecting partial knowledge and persistent legend.

### 5.2 The Cosmographiae and Natural Histories
Scholars like Sebastian Münster, in his *Cosmographia* (16th century), compiled geographic knowledge along with hearsay about monstrous beings. While they aimed for scientific explanation, these works often repeated older dragon stories, adding new "evidence" from recent travels. The result was a curious mix of genuine geographic detail and mythic creatures. Readers who studied such texts came away with a belief that dragons were part of the natural world, albeit in far-flung regions.

### 5.3 The Rise of Curiosity Cabinets
Nobles and wealthy merchants established "cabinets of curiosities" to showcase exotic items—shells, stuffed animals, rare plants, and sometimes alleged dragon remains. Explorers hoping to curry favor might present a "dragon's head" (usually a dried skate or ray manipulated to look monstrous) or large reptile eggs said to be from dragon nests. These displays fed the public's imagination and strengthened the conviction that real dragons existed, though typically far from Europe's well-explored lands.

---

## 6. Missionaries and "Dragon" Confrontations

### 6.1 Christian Accounts of Exorcism and Martyrdom
As Christian missionaries spread through Africa, Asia, and the Americas, some wrote letters describing how they encountered "devilish serpents" or "dragon idols." In attempts to convert local populations, they sometimes staged dramatic destructions of serpent effigies or held processions where they performed exorcisms of supposed dragon spirits. These theatrical events echoed the older tradition of saintly dragon-slaying, updated to new mission fields.

### 6.2 Negotiating Local Beliefs
Not all missionaries condemned foreign serpent deities outright. Some, influenced by Renaissance humanism, sought to understand local myths in cultural context. A Jesuit in China, for example, might view the Chinese dragon as symbolic of imperial virtue rather than a literal demon. Still, the official Church line generally identified any non-Christian spirit with demonic forces.

Written accounts from this period reflect tension between these more empathetic approaches and strict demonization.

### 6.3 The Propagation of "Dragon Tales"
Stories of missionary victories over "dragons" found receptive audiences in Europe. Publications promoted the Church's heroism abroad. Readers who devoured these accounts of spiritual warfare believed that the power of Christ had once again defeated the serpent, mirroring biblical narratives. Whether the "dragon" was a statue, a local ritual item, or a misunderstood large reptile, the printed pamphlets rarely distinguished. The outcome: a continued blending of actual encounters with animals or myths into sensational "dragon battles."

---

## 7. Skeptical Voices and Emerging Critiques

### 7.1 Early Skepticism
Alongside the fervor for dragons, a few intellectuals began questioning the literal existence of these monsters. Figures such as the physician Paracelsus (early 16th century) and some humanist scholars doubted travelers' wild claims. They suggested that sightings of dragons might be alligators, large snakes, or simply tall tales. Still, open disbelief was risky in a cultural environment where many forms of knowledge were shaped by tradition and religious authority.

### 7.2 The Influence of Empiricism
By the late 16th century, the seeds of a more empirical mindset were spreading among certain scholars and natural philosophers. These thinkers studied animal specimens systematically, trying to classify them in a logical framework. They argued that a beast as large and formidable as a true dragon would have left clearer evidence—captured specimens, consistent eyewitness reports. Some even traveled abroad to investigate "dragon sightings." Their findings often debunked sensational claims, concluding that explorers had mistaken crocodiles, giant lizards, or snake skins for dragons.

### 7.3 Tension Between Belief and Observation
Despite emerging skepticism, the broader public and many aristocratic patrons still delighted in marvels. So a curious dynamic arose: while a small circle of scholars pushed for naturalistic explanations, popular culture and official propaganda continued to favor thrilling stories of explorers facing dragons in Africa, Asia, or the New World. This tension persisted into the late 17th century, paving the way for more rational scrutiny in later eras.

## 8. The Role of Art, Theater, and Popular Literature

### 8.1 Illustrations and Woodcuts
Printed travelogues, such as those by Marco Polo's successors or other adventurers, often included woodcut images of serpents or "dragons" said to be found overseas. Artists exaggerated scales, wings, or horns to capture readers' imaginations. Though some images tried to be faithful to the traveler's notes, the lack of direct observation led to imaginative flourishes that shaped the public's mental picture of foreign dragons.

### 8.2 The Morality Play Tradition
In Europe, morality plays and pageants during festivals began inserting "exotic" dragons to represent evils from distant lands. These staged dragons sometimes breathed fire using primitive pyrotechnics, thrilling audiences who associated the Age of Exploration with discovering new horrors and temptations. The Church might sponsor such plays, using the dragon's defeat as a symbol of Christian and European triumph over pagan or unknown realms.

### 8.3 Adventure Narratives
The popularity of printed adventure narratives, including romances set against the backdrop of exploration, soared in the 16th century. Writers combined real geographic details—names of ports, descriptions of new fruits or customs—with imaginary battles against fearsome beasts. The line between fiction and travel reporting was often blurred. Readers eager for excitement devoured these tales, reinforcing the idea that true dragons still roamed faraway jungles, islands, or deserts.

---

## 9. Legendary Hoaxes and "Dragon Displays"

### 9.1 Faked Specimens
During this era, entrepreneurs found money in selling "dragon specimens" to curiosity-seekers. Some fashioned chimeric creations from dried fish parts or lizards, mounting them in grotesque poses. They claimed these were baby dragons captured abroad. Traveling fairs displayed these hoaxes, earning coin from onlookers. While some visitors likely believed they were seeing genuine creatures, others attended simply for amusement.

## 9.2 Royal Courts and Diplomatic Gifts

Foreign envoys sometimes presented unusual reptile skins or bones to European monarchs as diplomatic gestures. These gifts, described as "dragon remains," enhanced the mystique of a distant kingdom's wealth and power. Though some recipients suspected the items were crocodile hides or large serpentine skeletons, they often accepted them politely. Courtiers then showcased them in palace galleries, further embedding the notion that the Age of Exploration had uncovered actual dragons.

## 9.3 Impact on Collective Imagination

Such hoaxes and displays fed a feedback loop: the public, already primed by travel stories, saw "proof" in these oddities. The so-called dragon remains lent credibility to explorers' more sensational accounts. Even as rational thinkers questioned authenticity, large segments of society remained convinced dragons existed in unexplored territories, waiting to be discovered or defeated.

---

# 10. The Ongoing Fusion of Christianity and Dragon Lore

## 10.1 Continuation of Biblical Themes

Religious authorities in this period maintained that any monstrous reptile must be linked to demonic power. Sermons sometimes cited the explorers' or missionaries' "dragon encounters" as evidence that the devil still held sway in heathen lands. Converting those lands to Christianity was thus framed not only as saving souls but also as liberating them from the dragon's hold.

## 10.2 Saints, Martyrs, and New World Dragons

Some hagiographical works minted fresh narratives of saintly figures dealing with "heathen dragons" in the New World or Asia. Although these stories had minimal factual basis, they emulated the structure of older saint-dragon miracles. By retelling such sagas, the Church harnessed the dynamic sense of exploration to reaffirm its universal mission, casting priests and missionaries as modern dragon-slayers.

## 10.3 The Dragon as Colonial Allegory

In a broader sense, the image of slaying or taming dragons served as an allegory for colonization itself. European powers portrayed themselves as heroic knights confronting wild lands personified by dragons. Though not always explicit, this allegory justified conquest and Christianization, framing local resistance or unfamiliar cultural practices as monstrous or draconic. The result was a powerful mythic resonance that both guided and rationalized imperial expansion.

---

## 11. Cultural Exchanges and Hybrid Myths

### 11.1 Local Responses
Indigenous peoples in Africa, the Americas, and Asia had their own serpent and dragon-like tales. When faced with Europeans who insisted these were devils or literal beasts, local communities sometimes adapted their narratives to avoid persecution or reframe them for missionary ears. Over time, a hybrid myth could emerge, retaining some aspects of indigenous serpent lore but incorporating Christian or European dragon terminology.

### 11.2 Artistic Syncretism
Artistic depictions—whether in Christian churches established overseas or in local craft traditions influenced by European patrons—might show new forms of dragons blending local symbols with imported Western motifs. Examples include sculptures or paintings in mission churches that depict a saint triumphing over a serpent whose features combine local sacred animal traits with classic European draconic attributes.

### 11.3 Written Accounts by Non-European Observers
Some educated figures from Asia or the Americas traveled to Europe or wrote about their impressions. They noted how Europeans labeled certain reptiles as "dragons." A few critiqued the notion, pointing out that these were ordinary animals. Others found the European religious fascination with the devil as a dragon puzzling, especially if they came from a culture where dragons or serpent-gods were largely benevolent. Though these voices were fewer in the historical record, they highlight how the concept of "dragon" was not uniform but context-dependent.

---

# CHAPTER TWELVE: DRAGON SYMBOLISM IN HERALDRY AND ART

## Introduction

Medieval and Renaissance Europe used heraldry and symbolic art to express status, lineage, power, and moral ideals. Dragons played a central part in this visual language. Noble families adopted dragons on coats of arms to proclaim valor or ferocity, while churches and civic centers often included dragon motifs to represent spiritual or civic virtues (or to warn against evils). By the early modern period, dragons had migrated from bestiaries and legends to become key symbols in shields, banners, sculptures, and paintings across Europe.

In this chapter, we explore how dragons appeared in heraldic tradition, the rules and meanings behind those depictions, and the influence of both medieval lore and the Age of Exploration on their evolving designs. We also look at how dragons featured in monumental art—cathedral carvings, civic statues, and paintings that either honored heroic deeds or conveyed religious or moral lessons. From the flamboyant dragons of Renaissance prints to the austere serpentine gargoyles of Gothic cathedrals, we see how artists, patrons, and common folk alike used dragon imagery to communicate a rich range of ideas: chivalry, dominion, faith, fear, and even patriotism.

---

## 1. The Roots of Dragon Heraldry

### 1.1 Early Heraldic Traditions
Heraldry arose in medieval Europe as a system to identify knights on the battlefield, eventually extending to families, cities, and guilds. It relied on standardized designs (coats of arms) displayed on shields, banners, and surcoats. By the 12th century, geometric shapes and animal figures became common. Dragons—associated with might and mystery—naturally appeared among these symbols.

### 1.2 Dragons in Anglo-Saxon and Celtic Warfare
Before formal heraldry, Germanic war leaders sometimes carried "dragon standards," echoing Roman and possibly steppe nomad practices. The Bayeux

Tapestry (11th century) depicts some Norman or Anglo-Saxon banners with dragon-like figures. These were not yet "heraldic" in the strict sense but foreshadowed the use of draconic imagery to rally troops, signal lineage, or strike fear into foes.

### 1.3 Transition to Formal Heraldry

By the 13th century, heraldic authorities (kings of arms, heralds) began codifying design rules. Dragons quickly found a place: a knight who claimed descent from a legendary dragon-slayer or wanted to project ferocious bravery might adopt a dragon crest. Over time, certain lineages became strongly linked to these draconic arms, passing them down through generations.

---

## 2. Heraldic Variations of the Dragon

### 2.1 The Wyvern

In heraldry, the wyvern—a two-legged dragon with wings—appeared quite frequently. Some heraldic references distinguished the four-legged "true dragon" from the two-legged wyvern, assigning the latter slightly different symbolic traits. However, many heraldic artists used "dragon" and "wyvern" interchangeably. A wyvern on a shield could signify strength in battle, cunning, or dominion over the air and land.

### 2.2 The Basilisk and Cockatrice

Closely related to the dragon in heraldic tradition are the basilisk and cockatrice, reptilian hybrids sometimes depicted with a rooster's head. Though these creatures differ in bestiaries, medieval heraldry often grouped them with dragons under the general category of serpentine beasts. Their presence on a coat of arms might denote deadly power, often linked to the idea that the basilisk's gaze could kill.

### 2.3 Salamanders and Fire

While modern usage sees the salamander as an amphibian, medieval bestiaries described it as a creature that lived in fire. Some heraldic designs portrayed the salamander in flames, akin to a small dragon-like being impervious to heat. Although distinct from a dragon, this fiery salamander served a similar function: representing invincibility, courage, or purification through trial.

## 2.4 Color Symbolism

Heraldry relied heavily on color (tincture) symbolism. A dragon might appear in red (*gules*), signifying boldness or martial vigor; green (*vert*), representing fertility or nature's power; black (*sable*), hinting at cunning or sorrow; gold (*or*), denoting generosity or divine light. The chosen color shaped how viewers interpreted the dragon's significance on a given family crest or standard.

---

# 3. High Nobility, Royal Houses, and Dragon Emblems

### 3.1 The Welsh Dragon
One of the most famous dragon symbols in Europe is the red dragon of Wales. Tracing roots to early Celtic legends, it came to be associated with Cadwaladr ap Cadwallon, a 7th-century king, and later with the concept of Welsh nationhood. By the medieval period, the red dragon was firmly part of Welsh lore, sometimes used on flags or in literature like the *Mabinogion*. Over centuries, it became a proud emblem of resistance and cultural identity.

### 3.2 The Dragons of the Holy Roman Empire
Within the Holy Roman Empire, certain princely families included dragons in their arms to project strength or claim mythical ancestry. While the eagle was the empire's main symbol, local dukes or counts might adopt a dragon crest for personal or familial reasons. Some also borrowed from earlier Germanic dragon-slaying myths—Siegfried or related legends—folding those references into their heraldic narratives.

### 3.3 Eastern European Dynasties
In regions like Transylvania or Moldavia, heraldic dragons sometimes appeared, reflecting both local serpentine folklore and Western heraldic influence. The Order of the Dragon (founded by Sigismund of Luxembourg in the early 15th century) famously included Vlad II Dracul among its members, which contributed to the "draconic" theme in his family. Though overshadowed by later fictional works (such as the legend of Dracula in modern times, which we are not addressing here), the historical use of the dragon symbol by Vlad Dracul underscores the potency of draconic imagery for nobility.

### 3.4 Royal Orders and Dragon Decorations
European monarchs often established chivalric orders with distinct badges. The

Order of the Dragon, just mentioned, is one example. Knights wore medallions featuring coiled dragons, a sign of loyalty to the sovereign and commitment to defending Christianity against perceived threats (such as the Ottoman Empire at the time). These orders further elevated the dragon to a sign of elite martial and religious dedication.

## 4. Dragons in Civic and Guild Heraldry

### 4.1 City Emblems
Cities, too, embraced dragons in their arms or seals. Some medieval towns claimed legends of a local dragon once defeated by a founding hero or saint. Incorporating the dragon into the civic emblem reminded citizens of their shared history or moral lessons—good triumphing over evil. Others simply chose the dragon to symbolize strength, vigilance, or independence.

### 4.2 Merchant Guilds and Trade Companies
Some trade guilds or merchant associations used dragon symbols to project formidable presence overseas. During the Age of Exploration, as European merchants expanded globally, a guild crest featuring a dragon could imply boldness and readiness to face dangers—even mythical ones. The draconic imagery might appear on ships' figureheads, crates, or seals, reinforcing the group's identity.

### 4.3 Pageantry and Public Festivities
Cities often staged festivals or parades where large dragon effigies took center stage. These processional dragons could be puppets carried by multiple performers, sometimes spewing colored smoke or flames from hidden devices. The spectacle entertained crowds and reinforced civic pride. In some places, this tradition evolved from religious dragon-slaying plays into more secular celebrations of local lore.

## 5. Dragons in Religious Art and Architecture

### 5.1 Gargoyles and Stone Carvings
Medieval cathedrals are famous for their gargoyles—some depicting dragons or

dragon-like creatures. Functionally, gargoyles served as water spouts, but symbolically, they represented the malevolent forces outside the church's sanctuary. Their monstrous faces, including draconic snouts, reminded worshippers that sin and evil lurked in the world. Thus, the gargoyle or dragon on the cathedral roof was both a protective spirit (diverting water) and a moral lesson about the dangers of Satanic influence.

### 5.2 Altarpieces and Murals
Inside churches, dragons often appeared in depictions of saintly legends. Saint George slaying the dragon became a popular motif in altarpieces, stained glass, and frescoes. These works underscored the Christian message of good over evil. Other saints, like St. Margaret of Antioch, were likewise shown confronting dragons as a testament to their faith. The dragon's visual presence left no doubt about the spiritual conflict at stake.

### 5.3 Sculptural Reliefs and Tombs
Wealthy patrons sometimes commissioned tomb effigies or funeral monuments featuring draconic elements. A knight might be depicted resting with his foot on a subdued dragon, symbolizing the final triumph over sin, or representing heroic conquests in life. Bishops or abbots might have inscriptions referencing the dragon from the Book of Revelation, positioning themselves as defenders of the faith against the ancient serpent. In these ways, dragon imagery permeated not just the church's exterior but also the solemn memory of individuals within its walls.

---

## 6. Dragons in Secular Renaissance Art

### 6.1 The Flourishing of Allegorical Painting
By the Renaissance, artists like Paolo Uccello, Raphael, and others were painting vivid scenes of knights, saints, and mythological subjects. Dragons became a compelling element, allowing artists to showcase their skill in anatomy, perspective, and drama. In *St. George and the Dragon* paintings, the creature often took on stylized forms—part serpent, part winged beast—positioned to highlight the knight's poised heroism and the dynamic tension of battle.

### 6.2 Emblems and Decorative Motifs
Renaissance palaces and civic buildings might include ornamental friezes or

tapestries featuring dragons. Rulers commissioned these to display their might, sophisticated taste, or knowledge of classical mythology. Dragons could also appear in cameo reliefs, medal portraits, or goldsmith's work, symbolizing everything from martial prowess to alchemical transformation, depending on the patron's interests.

### 6.3 The Influence of Classical Revivals
With the Renaissance revival of Greek and Roman culture, older references to serpents—Typhon, Python, the Hydra—returned to prominence. Artists borrowed these classical motifs and combined them with medieval Christian dragon tropes. The result was a hybrid iconography: the dragon might be labeled a mythological Hydra but still carry moral undertones of sin or chaos. Humanists exploring ancient texts found new ways to interpret the dragon as an emblem of cosmic disorder subdued by reason or virtue.

## 7. Symbolic Interpretations and Shifting Meanings

### 7.1 Power, Dominance, and Fear
Whether on a coat of arms or a church sculpture, the dragon often symbolized power—both the fearsome might of the beast and the greater strength of the hero or saint who overcomes it. For nobles, adopting the dragon indicated a lineage unafraid of ferocious challenges. For religious art, the dragon's defeat highlighted the triumph of divine grace or moral virtue.

### 7.2 Transformation and Mystery
In some Renaissance circles, dragons also hinted at alchemical processes—transformation, hidden knowledge, and rebirth. Though these esoteric interpretations did not dominate mainstream heraldry or church art, they surfaced in private workshops or among intellectuals. Alchemical texts occasionally portrayed the dragon as matter to be refined, or as the dual nature of the material world that must be tamed to produce philosophical gold.

### 7.3 Regional Differences
The meaning of a dragon in heraldry or art varied across regions. In Italy, dragons might appear in reference to local saints (like St. John or St. Martha). In Germany, they might be tied to Teutonic heroism or local sagas. In Eastern Europe, they could evoke historical orders or militant traditions. These

variations show that while the dragon was universally recognized, its nuance depended on local legends and patron agendas.

## 8. The Dragon in Tournaments, Pageants, and Festive Culture

### 8.1 Jousts and Heraldic Displays
Chivalric tournaments featured knights wearing elaborate crests. A knight might mount a dragon effigy atop his helmet or have a surcoat embroidered with draconic motifs. Such displays were theatrical expressions of valor, linking the competitor to legendary beast-tamers. Painted shields and banners around the lists (tournament grounds) showcased families' arms, many of which included dragons.

### 8.2 Court Festivals and "Entries"
When a monarch or noble entered a city, local authorities often staged a triumphal procession with floats or mechanical beasts. A giant dragon might roll through the streets, spewing smoke. This spectacle entertained onlookers, while symbolically heralding the ruler's power to overcome chaos. Chronicles of these events describe lavish costumes, music, and scripted "battles" where a hero vanquished the dragon, paralleling the city's submission to the monarch's rule.

### 8.3 Plays and Masques
Court masques—dramatic entertainments combining dance, music, and allegory—often used dragons to represent disorder. A prince or allegorical figure would triumph over the dragon, signifying the harmonious rule of the sovereign. These performances borrowed from older religious pageants but placed the conflict in a secular or classical myth setting, showcasing the monarchy's glory and the sophistication of Renaissance art forms.

## 9. Reinterpretation During the Reformation and Counter-Reformation

### 9.1 Religious Conflicts and Dragon Imagery
The Reformation (16th century) sparked fierce conflicts across Europe. Protestant and Catholic propagandists alike used the dragon symbol to attack their opponents. Engravings might depict the pope or a Protestant leader as a dragon, or show a saintly figure slaying a serpent labeled "heresy." Dragon

metaphors that once exclusively symbolized the devil or pagan evil now targeted rival Christian factions, adding political meaning to the old device.

### 9.2 Iconoclasm and Art
Some Protestant movements, wary of religious images, destroyed or removed sculptures of saints slaying dragons from churches. Others retained them as historical or moral lessons but stripped away the overt Catholic context. Meanwhile, Catholic regions during the Counter-Reformation doubled down on dramatic visual art, sometimes amplifying the dragon motif to emphasize the Church's triumph over heresy. This polarization shows how flexible the dragon symbol could be: it served whichever side claimed righteous power.

### 9.3 Royal Patronage Continues
Despite religious tensions, European courts continued to sponsor grand artistic projects featuring dragons, whether for heraldic lineage or as an echo of medieval chivalry. Emblems once associated with feudal knights persisted as markers of aristocratic identity, bridging medieval and early modern aesthetics. Dragons, no longer purely medieval creatures, stayed relevant in evolving political and cultural contexts.

---

## 10. The Influence of Exploration on Heraldic Dragons

### 10.1 "Exotic" Elements Introduced
As covered in Chapter Eleven, the Age of Exploration introduced Europeans to new animals and foreign dragon-like myths. Some aristocrats, fascinated by travelers' accounts, began incorporating more "exotic" styles into their heraldic dragons—longer snouts, different scale patterns, or decorative motifs hinting at Asiatic or African influences.

### 10.2 Hybrid Crests
Certain families, especially those involved in overseas ventures, might fuse local heraldic tradition with references to far-off lands. A dragon's wings or tail might be stylized to resemble the creatures described in Indian or Chinese lore. While these details remained subtle in most cases, they reflected a growing awareness of dragons as a global phenomenon, not just a European legend.

### 10.3 Collectors and Artists Cross-Pollinating
Artists who studied foreign sketches or objects in curiosity cabinets sometimes

infused new designs into dragons for commissioned coats of arms or tapestries. For instance, a craftsman might see a Chinese dragon figurine, note its sinuous body and beard, and incorporate that aesthetic into a European-style dragon for a noble tapestry. Though such instances were limited, they illustrate how cross-cultural contact slowly expanded the visual vocabulary of dragons.

## 11. Lasting Legacy and Preparing for Change

### 11.1 The Enduring Popularity of Dragon Symbols
By the late 17th and early 18th centuries, Europe's heraldic traditions had peaked. Many noble families continued to display dragons in their arms, while cities and guilds cherished draconic emblems. Religious and moral art still depicted saints defeating dragons to affirm spiritual triumph. Public festivals kept rolling out dragon effigies to wow citizens. All these uses proved the dragon's deep grip on European imagination.

### 11.2 Seeds of Critique
Yet, as with the broader skepticism toward the literal existence of dragons, some intellectual circles began to see heraldic dragons as quaint relics of a bygone age. Enlightenment thinkers in the 18th century, favoring reason over medieval pageantry, might dismiss these symbols as superstitions. Others, particularly romantics, would later embrace them as part of Europe's noble heritage, celebrating the chivalric past.

### 11.3 Transition into Modernity
Though we are not moving into a full modern discussion, it's worth noting that by the end of the Renaissance, dragon symbolism in art and heraldry had already laid strong foundations for future reinterpretations. In the centuries that followed, some would cling to the medieval and Renaissance traditions as vital cultural symbols, while others would question or reimagine dragons in new creative forms. Regardless, the dragon as a heraldic and artistic device had cemented its place in European culture, bridging the gap between medieval chivalry, Renaissance creativity, and the global encounters of the exploration age.

# CHAPTER THIRTEEN: DRAGONS IN THE RENAISSANCE WORLD

## Introduction

The Renaissance, spanning roughly the 14th to the 17th centuries in Europe, was a period of extraordinary cultural and intellectual ferment. Scholars rediscovered classical texts, artists pursued realism and perspective, and thinkers expanded the boundaries of science and philosophy. During this time, dragons remained a key element in European imagination but underwent subtle changes in meaning and depiction. Earlier medieval views of dragons as diabolical monsters or symbols of evil persisted, yet the Renaissance fascination with the classical world, along with growing empirical curiosity, introduced new angles to the old dragon lore.

In this chapter, we examine how dragons featured in Renaissance scholarship, art, and literature. We will see how humanists reinterpreted classical serpents and monsters—like the Hydra or Python—in light of revived Greco-Roman texts, and how newly emerging scientific trends led some to question the existence of dragons altogether. Meanwhile, traveling artists, merchants, and missionaries continued to bring stories of "exotic dragons" from the East, blending them into Europe's shifting cultural landscape. By looking at these various strands, we gain a clearer picture of how Renaissance Europe reconciled its medieval inheritance with fresh ideas about nature, antiquity, and humanity's place in the cosmos.

---

## 1. The Humanist Revival and Classical Dragons

### 1.1 Rediscovery of Ancient Texts
Renaissance humanists, such as Petrarch and later scholars in Italy and beyond, delved into the works of Greek and Roman writers. They studied Homer, Hesiod, Ovid, and others, absorbing tales of serpents like the Hydra, Python, Ladon, and Typhon. These classical monsters, though somewhat different from medieval dragons, shared enough qualities—multiple heads, serpent-like bodies, cosmic conflict—that Renaissance readers often categorized them under the general heading of "dragons."

## 1.2 Mythological Interpretations

With humanism came an emphasis on allegorical and moral readings of classical myths. Scholars parsed accounts of Hercules slaying the Hydra or Apollo defeating Python, seeking moral or philosophical lessons within them. Some interpreters argued these beasts symbolized ignorance, chaos, or tyranny. Thus, the hero's victory over a serpentine monster could represent reason triumphing over superstition, a theme that resonated with Renaissance ideals about reviving classical learning and dispelling the "darkness" of the medieval past.

## 1.3 Influence on Renaissance Literature

Poets and playwrights drew on these classical sources to enliven their works. Italian epics like Ludovico Ariosto's *Orlando Furioso* (early 16th century) or Torquato Tasso's *Jerusalem Delivered* (late 16th century) included monstrous foes reminiscent of dragons or serpent-beasts. In these epics, the monstrous creature tested a knight's or hero's valor, echoing medieval chivalric traditions while injecting classical flair. The resulting blend—medieval Christian heroes battling classically inspired serpents—illustrates how the Renaissance bridged old and new, forging a hybrid culture in which dragons found fresh contexts.

---

# 2. Renaissance Art and the Dragon Motif

## 2.1 Evolving Aesthetics

Unlike the more stylized dragons of medieval art, Renaissance painters pursued anatomical accuracy and perspective. They attempted to depict dragons with realistic musculature, shading, and dynamic poses, even when referencing mythic or saintly scenes. Artists like Paolo Uccello, Raphael, and Tintoretto, among others, painted St. *George and the Dragon* or other heroic confrontations, displaying both mastery of form and dramatic tension. Though the subject was traditional, the artistic treatment reflected new standards of realism and emotional depth.

## 2.2 Classical Inspiration in Visual Depictions

Renaissance artists who studied ancient sculptures or Roman reliefs noted how classical serpents and griffins were depicted. Sculptors, influenced by the "rediscovery" of Greco-Roman statues, might carve dragons with distinct musculature or refined details, akin to a living creature. Some integrated decorative elements—like swirling scales or curling tails—that resembled classical motifs of sea serpents or monstrous hybrids found on ancient sarcophagi.

## 2.3 Symbolic Variety
Dragons in Renaissance art served multiple symbolic roles. In religious works, they remained a sign of evil or demonic power, subdued by saints or angels. In mythological paintings, they represented primal chaos or divine guardianship. In civic or courtly commissions, they displayed the patron's might or reference to legendary ancestry. Thus, while dragons had long been an emblem of fear and moral conflict, the Renaissance context opened up new allegorical possibilities—tying them to classical virtue, heroic lineage, or a demonstration of artistic virtuosity.

## 2.4 Patronage and Prestige
Wealthy patrons, including merchants in Florence or Venice, or royal courts in France and Spain, might commission large-scale works featuring dragons. A powerful noble could present himself as a "dragon-slayer," either literally (in epic-themed paintings) or metaphorically (showing victory over adversity). This dynamic expanded the dragon's function from purely moral or religious symbol to a statement of personal or political prestige, aligning with the Renaissance ethos of individual achievement and fame.

---

# 3. Scientific Inquiry and Growing Skepticism

## 3.1 Renaissance Natural Philosophy
The 15th and 16th centuries witnessed early stirrings of what would become modern science. Scholars like Leonardo da Vinci conducted anatomical studies, observed nature, and questioned inherited doctrines. They read classical authorities—Aristotle, Pliny—but also began to rely on firsthand observation. This shift from scholastic reliance on texts to empirical investigation had implications for belief in dragons.

## 3.2 Questioning the Existence of Dragons
As explorers brought back specimens of unusual reptiles—like iguanas, komodo-like monitors (though not yet precisely understood), or large snakes—some naturalists concluded that many so-called "dragon stories" arose from sightings of exotic but earthly creatures. They observed that if true dragons

existed, with massive size and wings, they should leave verifiable evidence. Absence of such proof prompted skeptics to label them myth or conflations of known animals, especially crocodiles.

### 3.3 Conrad Gessner and Other Encyclopedists
Works like Conrad Gessner's *Historiae Animalium* (1551–1558) tried to catalog all known animals, real and rumored. Gessner's approach was transitional: he included references to dragons as described in older sources, yet also noted that many travelers' tales lacked solid evidence. Illustrations in these early encyclopedias showed bizarre "dragon" forms, some clearly fictional. Readers could see side by side the new knowledge of lizards or large snakes next to medieval or classical dragon images, underscoring the uncertain boundary between recognized animals and legendary beasts.

### 3.4 Dissections and Hoaxes
A small circle of anatomists dissected alleged "baby dragons," discovering them to be rays, skates, or fabricated composites. Such hoaxes—often sold to curiosity cabinets—fueled further scrutiny. While the public still largely accepted that dragons might roam distant realms, leading natural philosophers in the major universities and courts grew more cautious, emphasizing direct observation and rational explanation. The seeds of a more critical view of dragons were thus firmly planted in the Renaissance period.

---

## 4. Courtly Masques, Festivals, and Theatrical Dragons

### 4.1 Lavish Spectacles
Renaissance courts indulged in theatrical events, including masques and pageants that showcased the era's creative flair. Dragons frequently appeared as stage props or mechanical contraptions, breathing fire or smoke. These illusions enthralled audiences, merging medieval pageantry with Renaissance artistry. Court inventors devised elaborate machinery—hidden bellows for smoke, wheels for movement—turning the dragon into a highlight of festivities.

### 4.2 Allegorical Roles
In these performances, the dragon often symbolized an obstacle to be overcome by a hero representing the prince or an allegorical figure of virtue. The subjugation or taming of the dragon might stand for the ruler's wise governance,

triumph over chaos, or moral leadership. Such spectacles flattered rulers and reinforced the idea that dragons, whether real or metaphorical, must bow to rightful authority.

### 4.3 Civic Celebrations
Outside royal courts, prosperous cities staged festivals involving giant dragon floats, echoing medieval traditions but now with Renaissance pomp. Artisans competed to design the most impressive "draconic" contraption. While older processions often carried religious significance—like St. George's feast day—Renaissance civic leaders sometimes used these events to celebrate economic success, forging a link between the city's prosperity and the grand spectacle of a subdued or friendly dragon.

---

## 5. The Printing Press and Spread of Dragon Narratives

### 5.1 Explosion of Printed Books
With Gutenberg's invention of the movable-type printing press in the mid-15th century, texts spread more widely than ever before. By 1500, printing presses operated in many European cities, producing books on history, geography, religion, and natural wonders. Dragons featured in multiple genres: bestiaries, travel accounts, legends, pamphlets, and allegorical treatises. This proliferation meant that even if actual dragons were in doubt, stories about them reached a larger audience.

### 5.2 Popular Pamphlets and Broadsheets
Printers also produced short pamphlets or single-page broadsheets with sensational headlines—"A Terrible Dragon Seen in the Alps!" or "Monstrous Serpent in the Plains of Hungary!" Many were unsubstantiated rumors, but they sold well. People eager for marvels devoured such accounts, reinforcing the idea that Europe still had pockets of wilderness where dragons might dwell, or that travelers beyond the continent might encounter them. Illustrations of supposed sightings, often crude woodcuts, gave the illusions a sense of authenticity.

### 5.3 Scholarly Disputes in Print
Meanwhile, academic circles debated the validity of dragon tales. Some scholars printed refutations, pointing to contradictory eyewitness reports or the absence of bodies. Others, more conservative or devout, maintained that Scripture

referenced dragons (especially in Revelation) and that saints battled them, so their existence was not to be questioned. Early printed books thus fueled both belief and skepticism, fostering a lively public conversation about dragons' reality.

## 6. Trade Routes, Merchants, and "Dragon Goods"

### 6.1 Exotic Imports
The Renaissance saw an expansion of trade routes linking Europe with Asia, Africa, and parts of the Americas. Merchants sometimes brought back items labeled "dragon teeth," "dragon scales," or "dragon blood." In reality, these might be crocodile teeth, pangolin scales, or the red sap known as "dragon's blood" (from the Dracaena plant). Yet, sold under the mystique of "dragon parts," they commanded higher prices and fed the belief that dragons were tangible.

### 6.2 Apothecaries and Medicinal Claims
In many Renaissance apothecaries, "dragon-based" remedies were advertised. Powdered "dragon bone" could be dinosaur fossils or large animal remains. "Dragon's blood" resin was used as a dye or medicine, believed to hold curative properties. Though some physicians began to question these claims, the older tradition—rooted in medieval bestiaries—remained compelling to many customers. The label "dragon" signaled potency and mystery, blending medieval herbal lore with Renaissance commerce.

### 6.3 Cultural Exchange and Dragon Iconography
Travelers to the Ottoman Empire, Persia, and beyond found local decorative arts featuring serpents, floral arabesques, or stylized dragon forms (influenced by Central Asian or Chinese motifs). These patterns sometimes made their way onto European ceramics, textiles, or metals, resulting in cross-cultural designs. While not always recognized as "dragon" by the original culture, European consumers often interpreted any sinuous, fierce-looking creature as a dragon, further spreading exotic styles at home.

# 7. Religious Tensions and Reform-Era Dragon Imagery

### 7.1 Continuation of Medieval Religious Themes
Despite the rise of humanism and rational inquiry, the Church still heavily influenced daily life. Scenes of St. George or St. Michael conquering dragons remained staples in church altarpieces and chapels. These images reminded believers of the cosmic battle against Satan. Reformers like Martin Luther (early 16th century) and the Protestant movement challenged certain Catholic practices, but they did not wholly reject biblical references to the dragon as evil. In Protestant regions, saintly or angelic dragon-slaying might be adapted to new theological contexts, focusing on Christ defeating sin.

### 7.2 Dragons in Religious Polemics
During the Reformation, Catholics and Protestants used dragon imagery in pamphlets and propaganda. Each side likened the other to a dragon—tyrannical, corrupt, or heretical. Woodcuts showed popes as seven-headed serpents, or reformist leaders as monstrous reptiles. These polemical images repurposed the well-known dragon motif to vilify opponents, bridging medieval demonization with the Renaissance print revolution's wide reach.

### 7.3 Counter-Reformation Art
In Catholic strongholds during the Counter-Reformation, the Church commissioned grandiose art to reaffirm doctrine and stir devotion. Dragon-slaying scenes grew more dramatic, painted with intense emotion and baroque flair. Caravaggio's followers, for example, might depict the moment of triumph with chiaroscuro lighting, accentuating the fearsome reptile writhing under the saint's spear. Here the dragon served not only as a general symbol of evil but also as a stand-in for Protestant heresy or the swirling chaos that threatened Catholic unity.

---

# 8. Patron Saints and Dragon Legends: Evolving Legends

### 8.1 St. George's Ongoing Prominence
St. George remained the most iconic dragon-slaying saint in Renaissance Europe, venerated in both Catholic and Orthodox regions. English tradition especially upheld him as a patron. With the spread of the printing press, his legendary story circulated in new forms—chapbooks, ballads—reinforcing the

image of a Christian knight conquering a monstrous dragon to save a maiden. Painters from the Low Countries to Spain produced countless variations of the famous scene.

### 8.2 Other Saintly Tales
Local cults of lesser-known saints also thrived. For instance, St. Martha (in French tradition) allegedly tamed the Tarasque, a dragon-like beast in southern France. Renaissance-era chroniclers elaborated on these older medieval tales, sometimes blending them with classical references or chivalric romance details. Thus, saintly feats from the Middle Ages were reframed in a more "Renaissance style," complete with classical architecture or humanist commentary on virtue.

### 8.3 Declining Literal Belief, But Lasting Allegory
Even as some educated nobles and clerics doubted the literal existence of dragons, these saintly legends endured for their allegorical power. Parishioners might no longer expect to see a living dragon in the countryside, yet the moral message of resisting evil or demonic forces stayed potent. The saint vs. dragon motif thus became less about actual monsters and more about spiritual or moral struggles—an evolution that would continue into the following centuries.

---

## 9. Renaissance Literature, Theater, and the Dragon's Role

### 9.1 Epic Poetry and Romance
Renaissance poets drew on the chivalric tradition in works like Ariosto's *Orlando Furioso* or Tasso's *Jerusalem Delivered*, where knights faced monstrous serpents or "dragons." These conflicts symbolized the hero's test of faith, love, or duty. Even Shakespeare, in a few passing references, invoked dragons to signify terror or might—though he mostly used them metaphorically. Overall, literary dragons during the Renaissance functioned less as straightforward fiends and more as dramatic embodiments of chaos, requiring a virtuous champion.

### 9.2 Moral Plays and University Drama
University students performed Latin plays or masques retelling classical myths. They staged battles with Hydra-like creatures or comedic dramas where a "dragon" represented ignorance, requiring a scholar to dispel it. The blend of medieval moral tradition (dragon as evil) with classical myth (dragon as

monstrous puzzle) showcased how Renaissance intellectual culture reimagined the old stories for academic or didactic entertainment.

### 9.3 Pastoral and Courtly Love Contexts
In some courtly or pastoral poems, the dragon might be portrayed sympathetically, or at least with complexity, reflecting the Renaissance taste for nuance. For example, a poet could compare unrequited love to taming a dragon—dangerous but potentially rewarding. While not mainstream, these poetic experiments foreshadowed later eras where dragons might appear as misunderstood or morally ambiguous creatures, rather than purely demonic forces.

---

## 10. Cross-Cultural Encounters and Shifts in Perspective

### 10.1 Arrival of Eastern Dragons in European Imagination
Renaissance travelers and missionaries in Ming China described imperial dragon motifs, noting that the Chinese revered dragons as benevolent, wise, and linked to royal authority. Jesuit letters home, like those of Matteo Ricci, sometimes marveled at Chinese art showing dragons controlling rain or representing cosmic harmony. Though overshadowed by more prominent religious or political concerns, these observations introduced a radical idea to Europe: not all dragons were evil.

### 10.2 Diplomatic Gifts and Curiosities
When Asian embassies or merchants visited European courts, they sometimes brought gifts featuring dragon designs—woven silks, porcelain, or carved jade. European courtiers admired the craftsmanship while puzzling over the friendly aspect of these dragons. Gradually, an alternative view of the dragon—graceful, wise, water-associated—began to filter into the Renaissance worldview, challenging the standard Western image of a monstrous serpent demon.

### 10.3 Broader Ethnographic Accounts
Some Renaissance geographers and writers included notes on indigenous serpent or dragon myths in the New World or Africa, gleaned from local sources. These might mention revered serpent spirits or protective water creatures. While heavily filtered through European assumptions, such accounts added diversity to the dragon concept. The wide variety of serpent beliefs worldwide,

from protective Nagas in India to the feathered serpents of Mesoamerica, led a few open-minded scholars to see dragons as a universal symbol with different cultural meanings, rather than a single monstrous entity.

## 11. Intellectual Tensions and the Road Toward Change

### 11.1 Tradition vs. Empirical Observation
By the late 16th century, Europe was increasingly divided between those who held to traditional lore—biblical references, saintly legends, bestiary heritage—and those who demanded verifiable evidence. Figures like Michel de Montaigne expressed cautious skepticism about miraculous tales. Others, especially in the universities, found themselves balancing piety and new scientific methods. Dragons lingered in the realm of uncertain wonders, neither fully discredited nor accepted as common animals.

### 11.2 Early Efforts at Classification
Naturalists like Ulisse Aldrovandi (16th century) tried to systematically categorize animals, including "dragons." Their works included drawings and textual descriptions, some based on third-hand stories. While Aldrovandi left room for real dragons, the struggle to place them alongside known reptiles signaled an emerging desire for taxonomic clarity. This push toward classification would intensify in the coming Enlightenment, further pressuring the concept of the dragon as an actual living species.

### 11.3 Cultural Resilience of the Dragon Image
Despite scholarly challenges, the dragon as a symbol remained robust. Public festivals, saint legends, heraldic crests, and popular pamphlets all kept the dragon alive in people's imaginations. Princes still used draconic emblems to evoke might, and preachers still invoked the dragon to represent the devil's cunning. Thus, even as certain educated circles questioned the literal existence of dragons, the creature's presence in daily life, art, and ceremony did not wane.

# CHAPTER FOURTEEN: DRAGONS DURING THE EARLY ENLIGHTENMENT

## Introduction

The Early Enlightenment, spanning from the late 17th to the early 18th centuries, brought sweeping changes to Europe's intellectual climate. Advances in astronomy, physics, biology, and other fields undermined older assumptions, urging scholars to rely on observation and reason rather than tradition and authority. In this era, leading figures like Isaac Newton, Robert Boyle, and Gottfried Wilhelm Leibniz spearheaded scientific pursuits, while philosophers such as John Locke and Voltaire questioned inherited beliefs. The period also saw the growth of scientific societies—like the Royal Society in England—that systematically investigated nature.

Against this backdrop, the status of dragons underwent further scrutiny. Were they genuine creatures lurking in unexplored corners of the globe, or relics of myth and superstition? While many common folk and even some aristocrats still accepted dragon lore, a growing number of thinkers pushed for empirical proof. Yet, the dragon did not simply vanish. This chapter examines how the Early Enlightenment shaped dragon discourse, through scientific inquiry, changing religious attitudes, continued folklore, and the first seeds of a romantic reinterpretation that would blossom in later centuries.

---

## 1. The Scientific Revolution and Dragons

### 1.1 The Rise of Empiricism
During the late 17th century, scholars increasingly used experimentation and careful observation to study the natural world. Francis Bacon's emphasis on inductive reasoning and the motto "Nullius in verba" (take nobody's word for it) from the Royal Society summarized the shift. Scientists tested claims by collecting specimens or performing experiments—an approach that favored tangible evidence over hearsay. Under these standards, the existence of dragons became harder to defend unless someone could produce a live specimen or incontrovertible remains.

## 1.2 Natural Histories and Cataloging

Naturalists like John Ray and Marcello Malpighi sought to classify plants and animals in systematic ways. Their efforts built on earlier compendiums but aimed for precision. If dragons were real, they would occupy a clear place in taxonomy. However, no reliable specimen ever emerged to allow such classification. By the turn of the 18th century, many scientific works relegated dragons to the "doubtful" or "mythical" category, explaining them as misidentifications of crocodiles, large snakes, or even fossil bones.

## 1.3 Fossil Discoveries and Speculation

Early paleontological finds occasionally sparked renewed curiosity about dragons. When large bones or teeth were unearthed, some wondered if they belonged to dragons. Yet scientists like Robert Hooke began to propose that these might be "petrified" remains of extinct creatures. Although the full theory of dinosaurs lay far in the future, these early fossil observations chipped away at the notion of living dragons. They also contributed to the idea that monstrous reptiles belonged to ancient epochs, not the modern world.

---

# 2. Scientific Societies and "Dragon Debates"

## 2.1 Royal Society, Académie des Sciences, and Others

Scientific societies formed across Europe in the 17th century. Their members wrote letters, presented findings, and sometimes debated sensational claims—like the sighting of a sea serpent or the capture of a "dragon." While a few members entertained such reports, the dominant mood favored skepticism. They demanded physical evidence, which rarely materialized beyond dubious "dragon skins" or repeated stories. Journals like the *Philosophical Transactions* might mention "dragon sightings," but typically in a critical tone, concluding there was insufficient proof.

## 2.2 Anatomical Investigations

When alleged dragons or "baby dragons" were brought to learned societies, anatomists examined them. Most turned out to be hoaxes. If genuine reptile specimens were large or unusual, they were identified as exotic lizards or amphibians. These methodical dissections further undermined the idea of a distinct dragon species. Nonetheless, rumors of living dragons in remote Asia or

Africa persisted, sometimes defended by travelers less bound by scientific standards.

### 2.3 "Wonders" vs. Natural Explanations

Natural philosophers widely dismissed the older bestiary tradition, calling it unscientific. The new approach sought rational, uniform laws of nature, leaving little space for a monstrous reptile that flouted known biology. This perspective contributed to a broader cultural shift: while "wonders" still fascinated the public, the educated elite increasingly explained them away as illusions, exaggerations, or phenomena with natural causes.

---

## 3. Changing Religious Context and Dragons

### 3.1 Evolving Theological Views

The Enlightenment did not erase religion; many thinkers were devout Christians or deists who believed in a Creator. But the once-dominant medieval worldview, where devils and demons roamed freely, was giving way to a more orderly cosmos governed by divine laws. Even in theology, emphasis on rational apologetics overshadowed older reliance on miracles and monstrous signs. The biblical references to "dragons" (Leviathan, Revelation's dragon) were reinterpreted as metaphors or poetic figures, not literal proof of living beasts.

### 3.2 Sermons and Moral Lessons

In many churches, pastors still invoked the dragon motif as an emblem of evil or sin. Yet they spoke of it more figuratively. Instead of claiming actual dragons lurked in the hills, they used the biblical serpent-dragon as an allegory for temptation or worldly corruption. The pious still believed that God had power over all creation, but fewer insisted that knights must remain vigilant for physical dragons hidden in forests.

### 3.3 Decline of Hagiographic Dragon Tales

Legends of saints defeating dragons lost some of their literal force, though they remained popular in religious art. During the Early Enlightenment, such stories were more readily admitted to be symbolic narratives representing spiritual warfare. Still, in rural areas, old traditions about local dragon stories could linger, retaining a degree of literal acceptance among those less exposed to Enlightenment teachings.

## 4. The Public's Continuing Fascination

### 4.1 Popular Culture vs. Scientific Circles
Despite the growing academic consensus that dragons were mythical, the general population—aristocrats, merchants, peasants—did not all adopt skeptical views overnight. Many lacked the scientific training or literacy to follow debates in learned journals. They continued to cherish folklore, chapbooks, and oral traditions describing dragons. Traveling fairs still showcased "dragon bones," and broadsheet publishers occasionally printed fresh reports of "winged serpents" terrifying remote villages.

### 4.2 Sensational Newspapers and Pamphlets
With the rise of early newspapers and pamphlets, sensational headlines about dragons maintained commercial appeal. Accounts from distant colonies or frontier areas could claim that local settlers had glimpsed monstrous reptiles. While more educated readers might scoff, these stories entertained a public eager for marvels. Some might half-believe them, especially if they distrusted the new "learned men" who seemed to undermine cherished beliefs.

### 4.3 Pageantry and Festivals
Cities and courts, continuing older traditions, staged festivals featuring mechanical dragons. Even if the intellectual elite doubted real dragons, the spectacle retained its cultural grip. People admired the skill of artisans who built these contraptions, and the pageant's narrative—hero slays dragon—still resonated as a celebration of communal or moral victory. Thus, the dragon's role in public life outlasted academic skepticism.

---

## 5. Folklore Collectors and Regional Dragon Myths

### 5.1 Early Folklorists
Toward the end of the 17th century and into the 18th, some scholars took an interest in collecting local folktales. They recorded legends of dragons in rural communities, preserving stories that had circulated for centuries. These accounts often featured half-historical details—like an ancient knight or bishop said to have slain a local "wyrm." While the collectors sometimes doubted the literal truth, they valued these tales as cultural heritage, marking one of the first steps in viewing dragon lore as part of folklore rather than natural history.

## 5.2 Transition from Belief to Legend
In many places, the idea of a real dragon menacing the region decades or centuries before started to shift from living tradition to legendary memory. Villagers might point to a hillside cave as the "dragon's lair," but fewer truly expected a dragon to emerge. The story's function had become a point of communal identity or a cautionary tale, bridging local pride and moral instruction, rather than a literal threat.

## 5.3 Documenting "Dragon Stones" and "Dragon Hills"
Folklorists noted how certain geological features—oddly shaped rocks, large caverns—were called "dragon stones" or "dragon hills." Locals explained these names with old stories of a dragon petrified by a saint's blessing or a beast burying treasure beneath a hill. Enlightenment-era travelers found these traditions quaint, seeing them as holdovers from a more superstitious past, yet recognized they enriched the cultural tapestry of the region.

---

# 6. Explorers and the Final Frontiers of Dragon Lore

## 6.1 Colonial Expansion and Exotic Reports
European powers continued expanding colonial territories in the 17th and early 18th centuries—North America, the Caribbean, parts of Africa, and Asia. Rumors of dragons in these areas persisted, particularly about the interior of Africa or uncharted swamps in the Americas. Explorers might relay claims from local peoples about giant snakes or spirit creatures. While some natural philosophers dismissed such reports as exaggerations, others kept an open mind, hoping to find the elusive proof.

## 6.2 Tales from Asia
In East Asia, particularly China and Japan, European traders and missionaries recounted ongoing local reverence for dragons. They described grand dragon parades, temple carvings, or imperial emblems. By the Early Enlightenment, Europeans increasingly understood that these "dragons" were not monstrous devils but cultural symbols of fortune and authority. While a few speculated about real serpent-like animals in Asia's interior, the main impression was that dragons there were revered mythic beings, far removed from European conceptions of evil dragons.

### 6.3 Diminishing Credibility of Dragon Sightings
Every so often, a traveler returned with a sensational "dragon story," but Enlightenment audiences demanded verification. If no solid evidence accompanied the claim—no specimen, no confirmed witness from a learned observer—journals and societies typically dismissed it. The systematic approach to geography, zoology, and anthropology left shrinking space for unverified wonders. Nonetheless, in popular travel literature aimed at general readers, dragons continued to appear as rhetorical flourishes or marketing ploys.

---

## 7. Enlightenment Philosophy and the Dragon as Symbol

### 7.1 Rationalist Critiques of Superstition
Philosophers like Voltaire ridiculed superstitions, including literal belief in dragons. They saw such notions as relics of ignorance. In their view, progress demanded casting off these childish fantasies. Yet, ironically, some used the dragon metaphorically to describe oppressive institutions—church or monarchy—as dragons devouring liberty. Thus, even in mocking real dragon belief, Enlightenment thinkers kept the image alive as a powerful allegory for tyranny or dogma.

### 7.2 Political Cartoons and Satire
Political cartoonists embraced the dragon motif to lampoon opponents. A politician might be depicted as a multi-headed dragon, signifying corruption or duplicity. Or a caricature might show the forces of reform slaying a dragon labeled "old regime." This usage paralleled earlier religious propaganda but now served a more secular, political message. The public, familiar with the longstanding symbol of a dragon as a formidable foe, recognized these cartoons' message instantly.

### 7.3 Poetic and Literary Shifts
As the Enlightenment advanced, some poets and writers began to treat dragons as purely mythical or romantic figures, reflecting on them as vestiges of a simpler time. They no longer promoted them as literal menaces but cherished them as part of Europe's cultural heritage—tales that stirred nostalgia or imaginative fancy. The stage was thus set for the later Romantic Movement, which would bring a resurgence of interest in medieval and mythical themes, dragons among them.

# 8. Continuing Devotional and Artistic Depictions

## 8.1 Baroque and Rococo Styles
In religious art, the baroque and rococo styles of the 17th and early 18th centuries emphasized ornate detail and dynamic movement. Dragon-slaying scenes grew more theatrical, with swirling draperies and dramatic lighting. St. George or St. Michael triumphing over a twisting serpent became a dramatic tableau, a swirl of color and motion. These pieces appealed to emotional intensity, even if some worshippers had grown less literal in their dragon beliefs.

## 8.2 Courtly and Architectural Flourishes
Secular architecture sometimes incorporated dragon motifs, especially in decorative friezes, garden statuary, or wrought-iron gates. For instance, a palace might feature carved dragons flanking the main entrance, symbolizing vigilance or echoing the noble family's heraldic arms. Even as scientific circles questioned dragons' existence, aristocratic taste for grandeur used their fierce shapes for visual impact. The dragon retained an aura of awe, bridging the whimsical and the imposing.

## 8.3 Opera and Musical Theatre
Early opera, emerging in the late 16th century and flourishing in the 17th and 18th, frequently tackled mythological or heroic subjects. A stage dragon might appear in an opera about Hercules, Perseus, or a saintly story. Mechanized stage props allowed for illusions: a dragon might "fly" overhead or breathe fire with pyrotechnics. Audiences enjoyed the spectacle, less concerned about real biology than the dramatic effect of the monstrous reptile in a grand musical setting.

---

# 9. Learned Debates: Myth, Allegory, and Proto-Folklore Studies

## 9.1 Antiquarians and Classical Comparisons
Antiquarians studied ancient coins, inscriptions, and art, noticing serpentine creatures akin to dragons across different cultures. Some proposed that "dragon" myths originated as allegorical stories about natural disasters—volcanoes or floods—or as symbolized political struggles. This historical-linguistic approach foreshadowed modern mythological analysis, where the dragon becomes a cross-cultural symbol rather than an actual beast.

## 9.2 Early Rationalizing Theories

A few Enlightenment writers ventured rationalizing theories: perhaps "dragon battles" recounted by saints were historical accounts of heroes killing large crocodiles or pythons. These theories served to preserve a kernel of truth in the legend—there might indeed have been a dangerous reptile—while explaining away supernatural elements. Although not universally accepted, such rationalizations signaled a shift toward seeing mythology as metaphor or distortion of real events rather than literal fact.

## 9.3 Pre-Romantic Fascination

Toward the early 18th century, a subset of intellectuals developed a fascination with medieval chivalry and old legends. While still part of the Enlightenment world, they appreciated the imaginative power of tales about dragons and knights. This minority view set the stage for the Romantic Movement's later embrace of the "Gothic" and the "medieval," where dragons would reappear with renewed vigor in literature and art.

---

# 10. The Fate of Dragons in Colonial Domains

## 10.1 Indigenous Beliefs and European Interpretations

In colonial territories, European officials sometimes took local serpent or crocodile cults as evidence that "dragon worship" persisted among "uncivilized" peoples. Enlightenment-era administrators, though less prone to religious condemnation, might still record these practices as curious remnants of ancient superstition. Meanwhile, local communities had their own traditions, occasionally adopting the European term "dragon" to describe certain spirit-animals or revered reptiles, leading to cross-pollination of lore.

## 10.2 Missionaries and Cultural Conflict

Missionaries continued to interpret serpentine deities as demonic. Yet the Enlightenment's emphasis on rational persuasion influenced some mission strategies. Rather than framing everything as devils, certain missionaries attempted to scientifically "prove" that revered serpents were mere animals, unworthy of worship. This approach clashed with local spiritual perspectives, adding a new dimension to the long-standing tension over "dragon-like" beliefs.

### 10.3 Collectors of Curiosities Overseas

Enlightenment-era travelers sometimes returned with alleged "dragon artifacts"—skins, claws, or horns purchased from local markets—just as earlier explorers had done. But now, scientific societies often examined these items. If found fraudulent, they were dismissed. A few genuine oddities, such as large reptile hides from Komodo dragons (not widely recognized as such at the time), contributed to the partial acknowledgment that some very large lizards did exist—though still not the winged, fire-breathing dragons of old.

---

## 11. Shifting Cultural Perceptions by the Mid-18th Century

### 11.1 Dragons as Fictional Monsters

By the mid-18th century, a consensus had emerged among European intellectuals: dragons were not real creatures. They had become "literary monsters," preserved in folklore, epic tales, and religious iconography, but absent from serious zoological catalogs. In fact, a well-educated person might find it quaint or backward to assert actual dragon sightings. The creature's realm was now that of legend, metaphor, or at best, unknown extinct species.

### 11.2 Persisting Rural Beliefs

However, not everyone read scientific journals or embraced Enlightenment rationalism. In more isolated rural regions, local legends persisted as living tradition. Farmers might still recount how their grandparents encountered a lurking wyrm near a cave, or how an old saint once banished a scaly fiend from the village well. Such stories no longer carried the same unanimous acceptance they once did, but they remained part of communal identity.

### 11.3 The Coming Romantic Reassessment

As the Enlightenment gave way to the late 18th century, signs of an intellectual shift appeared. Some poets and artists were weary of pure reason and yearned for mystery, emotion, and the medieval aesthetic. Dragons, along with ghosts and ancient ruins, began to evoke a romantic longing for a past rich with wonder. Though this sentiment would fully blossom in the 19th century, the seeds were planted in the Early Enlightenment, ensuring that the dragon would not fade from cultural consciousness but simply adopt new roles.

---

# CHAPTER FIFTEEN: DRAGONS IN THE COLONIAL ERA

## Introduction

From the mid-18th century through much of the 19th century, European powers expanded their colonial reach across Africa, Asia, the Americas, and the Pacific. This "Colonial Era" (loosely spanning the late Enlightenment into the early Industrial period) saw massive shifts in politics, economics, and cultural interactions. During this time, the old question of dragons—whether they were real animals, symbolic monsters, or purely mythical beings—did not vanish. Instead, it evolved under the pressures of scientific thought, colonial policy, missionary activity, and cross-cultural exchange.

In this chapter, we explore how colonial encounters shaped and were shaped by the lingering lore of dragons. We will see how missionaries still framed certain local serpent deities as "dragons" to be combated, how some colonists used dragon imagery to symbolize conquest or dominion, and how newly founded scientific institutions in colonial territories evaluated claims of local "dragons." We also examine how indigenous peoples responded, sometimes adapting the "dragon" label to their existing serpent traditions or rejecting it as alien. Finally, we delve into how travelogues, museum displays, and early anthropology contributed to a growing Western consensus: that living dragons did not roam the earth—yet the concept of the dragon remained culturally potent as an emblem of the strange and the exotic.

---

## 1. The Colonial Landscape and Prevailing Attitudes

### 1.1 European Imperial Expansion
By the mid-18th century, European maritime powers—Britain, France, Spain, Portugal, the Netherlands, and others—controlled vast overseas territories. Colonies in the Americas were well established, while expansions in India, Southeast Asia, and parts of Africa accelerated. The Age of Reason shaped the administrative frameworks of these colonies, emphasizing the gathering of knowledge: mapping lands, documenting flora and fauna, and classifying indigenous societies. Dragons (or rumored monstrous reptiles) sometimes

surfaced in colonial reports, but the official stance among most colonial authorities leaned toward skepticism.

### 1.2 Shifting Intellectual Climate
Building on the Enlightenment's momentum, European elites in the late 18th and early 19th centuries increasingly prized empirical data. Universities taught natural history and geology, while learned societies continued to publish scientific findings. Although pockets of tradition and popular belief still existed, official knowledge channels were dominated by rationalism. Within this rational climate, claims of real dragons in the colonies were often met with demands for physical proof.

### 1.3 The Function of Dragon Lore in Colonial Culture
Nevertheless, the idea of dragons retained appeal in certain circles. Some colonists romanticized exotic lands as realms where fantasy might be real. Others used the notion of monstrous reptiles to justify "taming" or "civilizing" untamed wilderness. Missionaries drew on biblical images of the dragon as a demon, describing local serpent cults or spirit beliefs in dramatic, moralizing terms. Thus, even as scientific frameworks prevailed, the colonial environment allowed for a variety of dragon-related narratives to flourish and clash.

---

## 2. Missionary Perspectives and Conflicts

### 2.1 "Heathen Dragons" in Missionary Texts
Missionaries, both Catholic and Protestant, spread widely across Africa, Asia, and the Pacific. In their letters home and published mission reports, some described local deities or revered serpents as "dragons." For example, a West African python cult or an Indian naga shrine could be recast in Christian pamphlets as "dragon worship," echoing medieval traditions of saints destroying serpent idols. While such language might not reflect actual local beliefs, it served to dramatize the missionary's struggle against perceived paganism.

### 2.2 Attempts to Reenact Saintly Dragon-Slaying
Certain zealous missionaries staged symbolic battles—destroying serpent effigies or burning sacred groves—presenting themselves as modern-day saints vanquishing "dragons" of superstition. Reports of these events circulated in church newsletters, captivating European congregations. The same motif

reappeared in sermons or devotionals, painting the missionary as a heroic champion confronting a monstrous evil. Over time, however, these accounts drew criticism from more moderate church leaders who saw them as sensationalist or disrespectful of local cultures.

### 2.3 Indigenous Responses

From the perspective of indigenous communities, the missionary labeling of revered serpents as "dragons" was often perplexing. Local beliefs about serpents might see them as ancestors, guardians of water sources, or symbols of fertility. The Christian condemnation and destruction of such symbols could create cultural rifts. In some cases, leaders or healers adapted to the new environment—perhaps acknowledging a "dragon" label but maintaining deeper spiritual ties to the serpent figure. In others, violent confrontations erupted. Thus, the missionary crusade against "dragons" fed into broader colonial tensions, shaping cross-cultural encounters with layers of misunderstanding and resistance.

---

## 3. Colonial Administration and Scientific Investigation

### 3.1 Colonial Offices and Natural History

European colonial administrations often funded surveys of local geography, resources, and wildlife. Naturalists joined expeditions into unfamiliar regions, collecting specimens for museums back home. If local rumors spoke of monstrous reptiles or "dragons," these naturalists might investigate. However, they typically approached such rumors with skepticism, looking for known species (pythons, monitor lizards, crocodiles) that might have sparked exaggerated tales.

### 3.2 Founding of Museums and Collections

During the late 18th and early 19th centuries, major museums in London, Paris, Vienna, and other capitals expanded their collections with exotic specimens from the colonies. Curators compiled anatomical data, while some large reptiles—stuffed crocodiles or pythons—were occasionally displayed under the label "dragon" as a crowd-pleasing curiosity, even if scientifically they were recognized as standard reptiles. The general public visiting these institutions might walk away believing that dragons, in some sense, existed, though the scholarly text would clarify that these were real animals incorrectly lumped under the mythical name.

### 3.3 Disproving Dragon Myths on the Ground

Some colonial governors or officers sought to pacify local fears by disproving rumored "dragons." If peasants refused to farm near a swamp because a "dragon" was said to dwell there, an official might dispatch soldiers or naturalists to flush out whatever crocodile or large snake lurked within. Reports of these efforts found their way into official gazettes, championing the rational triumph of colonial authority over local superstition. In doing so, the administration reinforced its own legitimacy—positioning the colonial government as a force that banished monstrous threats.

---

## 4. The Role of Travelogues and Adventure Literature

### 4.1 Popular Demand for Exotic Tales

The reading public in Europe continued to devour travelogues—accounts of explorers, traders, and soldiers describing distant lands. Publishers discovered that exotic creatures, including rumored dragons, sold books. While more sober texts downplayed such claims, many adventurers capitalized on them. A traveler's memoir from Southeast Asia might include a chapter about "the dragon of the swamp," retelling local legends with dramatic flair. Even if the author personally believed it to be a crocodile, the dragon label made for a thrilling chapter.

### 4.2 Romanticized Colonial Adventures

By the early 19th century, a budding romantic sensibility prized the mysterious and the sublime. Writers of colonial adventures played into this, framing jungles, deserts, and mountains as domains where old European legends—like dragons—took on new life. A swashbuckling hero might "battle a dragon" in Africa, only for the text's footnote to explain it was likely a giant monitor lizard. But the narrative was less about scientific accuracy and more about conjuring a sense of danger and wonder.

### 4.3 Illustrations and Engravings

Illustrated travel books sometimes featured engravings of monstrous reptiles. Artists based these scenes on secondhand descriptions or their own imaginations, often exaggerating the creature's size or adding draconic traits like wings or spines. The result: a portion of the public still thought dragons might lurk in remote corners of the colonial world. These images circulated widely, further blurring the line between genuine zoology and mythic re-creation.

## 5. Cross-Cultural Interplay: Local Serpent Deities and the "Dragon" Label

### 5.1 African Spiritual Traditions
Across Africa, various ethnic groups revered water spirits or serpentine beings linked to fertility, rain, or clan ancestors. European colonists or missionaries often lumped these beings together under the label "dragon," especially if local artwork showed a large snake with anthropomorphic or supernatural features. In reality, African spiritual cosmologies were complex, with serpents symbolizing everything from healing to transitions between realms. The foreign "dragon" label sometimes stuck in colonial records, leading to misunderstandings about local religious systems.

### 5.2 Indian and Southeast Asian Nagas
In India, the naga tradition persisted, with serpent deities occupying temples and shrines. British or French colonial officers might note these as "dragon shrines," continuing a centuries-old confusion from earlier travelogues. Meanwhile, in Southeast Asia, stories of naga or giant serpents controlling rivers also faced the colonial reinterpretation. Local communities adapted or resisted. Some took advantage of European curiosity by selling "naga relics"—bones or scales from large fish—re-labeled as "dragon parts" for eager collectors.

### 5.3 Chinese and East Asian Dragons
By the Colonial Era, Europeans in China encountered a refined tradition of dragon symbolism: the imperial dragon on flags, palaces, and official garments. As Western powers tried to open trade or force concessions, they engaged with these symbols. Missionaries too encountered elaborate dragon motifs in festivals or religious processions. While mainstream Western science dismissed the existence of literal dragons, some merchants played up the "mysterious East" angle in stories aimed at Western audiences, describing the Chinese dragon as an actual creature. This added to the romantic aura of Asia as a land of living myth, though more rigorous sources recognized the dragon as a revered cultural emblem, not a physical beast.

## 6. Dragons, Colonial Power, and Symbolic Dominance

### 6.1 "Slaying the Dragon" as Colonial Metaphor
In certain propaganda, dragons became stand-ins for rebellious territories or the "barbarous customs" colonists aimed to eradicate. Newspapers or political

cartoons depicted a British or French soldier as a knight confronting a native "dragon," signifying the struggle to impose colonial rule. Such imagery echoed older medieval tropes but repurposed them for an era of empire-building. Conquering the "dragon" equated to subjugating lands considered wild or resistant.

## 6.2 Emblems on Colonial Flags or Crests
A handful of colonial ventures adopted draconic imagery in flags, seals, or military insignia. For instance, a local militia in a particular colony might stylize a winged serpent on its banner, referencing either the mother country's heraldry or local legends. While not widespread, these examples illustrate how the dragon retained symbolic power for representing both might and the mysterious.

## 6.3 Resistance and Indigenous Symbolism
On the other side, some indigenous leaders appropriated or adapted dragon imagery—especially if European discourse equated local serpents with the dreaded beast. By turning the "dragon" label into a mark of pride or defiance, they inverted the colonial metaphor. This dynamic was less common but did occur in pockets of syncretic rebellion, where local communities embraced the monstrous label bestowed by colonizers to assert their own identity and resilience.

---

# 7. Missionary Schools and Education: Teaching Dragons as Myth

## 7.1 Curriculum in Colonial Schools
Colonial administrations established schools for indigenous elites or broader populations. In missionary-run institutions, biblical narratives involving serpent-dragons (like references to Revelation or saintly legends) were taught alongside geography, basic science, and Western history. Teachers generally emphasized that real dragons did not exist, though the biblical "dragon" symbolized evil. This approach sought to impart rational knowledge while maintaining Christian moral allegories.

## 7.2 Indoctrination or Enlightenment?
Opinions varied. Some viewed these schools as vehicles of enlightenment, freeing local youth from "superstitious beliefs" in monstrous serpents. Others saw them as indoctrination, eroding traditional lore and overshadowing local

serpent myths with a Western perspective. Either way, the missionary-school environment contributed to a gradual shift: younger generations in colonial regions increasingly regarded the "dragon" not as a literal being but as a Christian or Western cultural figure.

### 7.3 Hybrid Folktales in Classroom Context
In some colonial schools, students or teachers combined elements: local serpent stories were retold through a Christian lens, labeling them "dragons" vanquished by faith, or they were explained away scientifically. Over time, these hybrid narratives filtered back into local communities, resulting in new forms of legend that blended indigenous symbolism with the colonial demonization—or rational dismissal—of monstrous reptiles.

---

## 8. Newspapers, Broadsheets, and Colonial Gossip

### 8.1 Reports of "Dragon Sightings"
In colonial towns, newspapers carried sensational stories about "dragon sightings" in the nearby jungle or savanna. The subject proved irresistible for editors seeking readership. Such articles typically began with breathless claims, describing a winged beast terrorizing villagers. Follow-up pieces often revealed a large python or monitor lizard. Yet the initial thrill overshadowed the debunking. So, rumors persisted, fueling local lore.

### 8.2 Travel Warnings and Tall Tales
European settlers traveling between remote outposts sometimes swapped exaggerated "dragon stories" around campfires to entertain or frighten newcomers. Guides or native porters might feed into these stories for amusement or to deter explorers from venturing into culturally sensitive areas. Colonial authorities sometimes had to issue statements clarifying that no dragons roamed the territory, though ironically such proclamations could stir curiosity further.

### 8.3 Merchants and Dragon Merchandise
Entrepreneurs capitalized on the dragon mystique, selling "dragon oil," "dragon bone powder," or curios claiming draconic origins. Tourists or traveling colonists snapped them up as exotic souvenirs. While many recognized these items as novelty, some believed in their medicinal or protective properties. This trade

paralleled earlier eras but thrived under the colonial market system, distributing "dragon goods" far beyond local communities to new consumer bases in Europe and other colonies.

## 9. The Emergence of Early Anthropology and Ethnography

### 9.1 Studying Indigenous Beliefs
By the early 19th century, a nascent field of anthropology began taking shape. Colonial officials, missionaries, and scholars recorded local customs with more systematic methods—sometimes aiming to classify cultures in a hierarchical framework. In these accounts, references to serpent worship or monstrous creatures frequently appeared. Writers debated whether these beliefs indicated "primal superstition" or sophisticated symbolic systems. Dragons were often invoked as a conceptual bridge, equating local serpents with Western mythical beasts.

### 9.2 Shifting Interpretations
A few enlightened thinkers tried to interpret serpent or "dragon" lore within its indigenous context, appreciating the spiritual or ecological significance it held for the community. These ethnographic attempts might note how local stories about giant serpents aligned with real ecological concerns, such as protecting water sources or respecting wildlife. Such sympathetic approaches were overshadowed, however, by mainstream colonial attitudes that saw these beliefs as quaint or backward.

### 9.3 Dissemination Through Ethnographic Journals
Ethnographic findings circulated in journals read by scholars and colonial administrators. Articles might detail an African tribe's "dragon dance" or a Polynesian "dragon deity," often laced with paternalistic language. Nonetheless, the act of documentation preserved valuable details about local serpent traditions that might otherwise have been lost under colonial pressure. Inadvertently, these journals contributed to a broader understanding that "dragon" was a flexible category spanning multiple cultures and contexts.

# 10. Literary Trends: The Colonial Dragon in Fiction and Poetry

### 10.1 Romantic Colonial Narratives
During the early 19th century, Romantic literature soared in Europe, exalting nature, emotion, and the sublime. Some novelists set stories in far-off colonies, weaving in local legends of monstrous serpents as romantic or terrifying backdrops. The "colonial dragon" thus became a literary trope—part exotic spectacle, part metaphor for the vast unknown. These works, though fictional, shaped how home audiences imagined the colonies.

### 10.2 Poetic Themes of Conquest and Wonder
Poets, too, invoked dragons to symbolize the tension between raw wilderness and the civilizing mission. A poem might describe a heroic settler grappling with a scaly horror in a tropical forest, capturing the emotional extremes Romanticism prized. Alternatively, a poet might bemoan the destruction of indigenous serpent traditions, lamenting the loss of mystery under relentless colonial rationalism. Such verses highlight how dragons served multiple rhetorical functions: conquest, wonder, destruction, or cultural clash.

### 10.3 Children's Stories and Colonies
Some children's books used colonial settings as stage sets for juvenile adventures, featuring friendly or fearsome "jungle dragons." These imaginative tales overshadowed real ethnographic detail but fed into a youthful fascination with the exotic. As a result, younger readers in Europe developed strong mental links between dragons and far-flung colonial worlds, long after scientific consensus had abandoned the notion of living dragons.

---

# 11. Native Adaptation and Resistance

### 11.1 Local Mythic Evolution
In certain colonized regions, indigenous storytelling adapted the "dragon" idea for local ends. A serpent deity might adopt new attributes gleaned from missionary or colonial demonology—growing wings, breathing fire, or battling a saint. Over generations, a unique "hybrid dragon" legend emerged, reflecting both local traditions and imported motifs. This process was not always passive: storytellers actively reshaped foreign elements to preserve or reassert cultural identity.

## 11.2 Rebellions and Dragon Emblems
Occasionally, rebel factions adopted a "dragon banner" or invoked a serpent spirit in uprisings against colonial powers. By presenting themselves as champions of a fearsome, ancient force, they aimed to rally popular support. The colonial authorities often dismissed such symbolism as savage or childish, but for those in rebellion, it channeled ancestral pride. These examples underscore how the "dragon," once used to vilify indigenous beliefs, could become a sign of defiance.

## 11.3 Cultural Brokers and Interpreters
A small class of indigenous intellectuals fluent in European languages sometimes functioned as cultural brokers. They explained local serpent stories to colonial scholars, or conversely, introduced the concept of the "European dragon" to their own communities. Their interpretations varied—some embraced scientific skepticism, while others found parallels between the European "dragon" and local protective serpent deities. This interplay shaped newly emerging syncretic mythologies.

---

# 12. Declining Credibility and the Path Toward the 19th Century

## 12.1 Accumulated Evidence Against Dragons
By the early 19th century, systematic exploration and zoological study across colonies yielded a vast catalog of species. None corresponded to the traditional fire-breathing, winged dragon. While large reptiles (komodo dragons, monitor lizards, giant anacondas) impressed observers, they fell squarely into established biological categories. The argument that a true dragon might still lurk undiscovered lost credibility, especially among scientifically minded officials and scholars.

## 12.2 The Transformation of the Dragon's Image
As rational skepticism took hold, the dragon shifted further from a potential living creature to an emblem in art, literature, or morality tales. Missionary zeal to "slay dragons" in pagan lands quieted somewhat, replaced by more nuanced approaches to evangelism or by secular colonial administration. Meanwhile, the broader European public, enthralled by industrial progress, came to see dragons as part of a fading medieval or purely imaginative realm—though colonial exoticism still occasionally revitalized the old fantasy.

### 12.3 Seeds of Later Romantic Fascination

Toward the close of the Colonial Era's early phases, an undercurrent of Romanticism had begun to cast the dragon in a nostalgic or heroic light. Writers and artists back in Europe, disillusioned with unbridled rationalism, turned to folklore for inspiration. Some found fresh impetus in colonial travelogues that alluded to serpent gods. The stage was set for the 19th century's deeper dive into folklore, nationalism, and imaginative revival, where dragons would reemerge as central figures in cultural identity and romantic fantasy.

---

## 13. Museums, Exhibitions, and the Public's Perception

### 13.1 World's Fairs and Showcasing the Exotic

The late 18th and early 19th centuries saw precursors to large-scale exhibitions or fairs. Although the famous "World's Fairs" proper belong mostly to the mid-19th century, earlier colonial exhibitions displayed curiosities from overseas: stuffed beasts, cultural artifacts, and re-enacted "tribal villages." Occasionally, a "dragon skeleton" or "dragon skin" appeared, fueling spectacle. Organizers typically framed these items as marvels from savage lands. While official notes might clarify they were crocodile remains, the sensational press coverage still used the word "dragon."

### 13.2 Changing Attitudes Among Urban Audiences

Urban populations in European capitals, exposed to museum collections and exhibitions, increasingly recognized the difference between legitimate zoological finds and mythical beasts. Over time, curiosity about "dragon remains" yielded to interest in genuine species classification. Nonetheless, many visitors still delighted in the romantic illusions, wishing for a shred of reality behind the old legends.

### 13.3 Traveling "Dragon Shows"

Entrepreneurs took advantage of colonial lore by staging traveling shows—small circuses or cabinets of wonder that claimed to exhibit dragons. Dried stingrays, plaster models, or manipulated reptile corpses formed the main attractions. In smaller towns, these shows might still convince spectators, but in major cities with established museums, they faced more suspicion. Yet even a skeptical audience sometimes paid for the thrill of seeing a "dragon," half-knowing it was a trick but savoring the mystique.

# CHAPTER SIXTEEN: DRAGONS IN NINETEENTH-CENTURY FOLKLORE

## Introduction

The 19th century was an era of dramatic change. Revolutions and reform movements reshaped politics, while the Industrial Revolution and advances in science continued to transform daily life. In the realm of cultural identity, a growing romantic nationalism gripped Europe and beyond, inspiring people to look back at their own past—myths, legends, and folklore—for meaning and unity. Dragons, once dismissed by many Enlightenment thinkers as relics of superstition, reemerged in new guises: as cherished symbols of national heritage, as intriguing subjects for the blossoming fields of folklore and comparative mythology, and even as potential links between legend and emerging paleontological science.

In this chapter, we examine how dragons resurfaced in 19th-century folklore studies, art, literature, and nascent scientific discourse. We look at the romantic rediscovery of medieval epics, the compilation of local legends by folklorists, the creation of new fairy tales featuring dragons, and the influence of paleontological findings that encouraged some to wonder if dragon stories held prehistoric echoes. By century's end, dragons had moved away from being literal menaces to become beloved cultural icons, potent romantic images, and occasionally, tantalizing puzzle pieces hinting at Earth's ancient past.

---

## 1. The Romantic Movement and Medieval Revival

### 1.1 Romantic Nationalism and the Search for Roots
Across 19th-century Europe, a wave of romantic nationalism spurred interest in folk traditions, medieval epics, and historical myths. Intellectuals and artists sought authentic cultural identities distinct from the cosmopolitan Enlightenment. They idealized an older, more "organic" past, free from industrialization and rational strictures. In the process, they revived interest in epic sagas—such as the Nibelungenlied in German-speaking lands or the Arthurian cycle in Britain—many of which included dragons or dragon-like foes.

## 1.2 Medieval Epics and the Dragon's Return

As translations and popular editions of medieval works flourished, the dragon reemerged in popular culture. Stories of Beowulf's final battle with a dragon, or Sigurd (Siegfried) slaying Fafnir, gained fresh attention. Scholars annotated these texts with historical and philological commentary, while artists produced new illustrations capturing the romantic grandeur of knights battling serpentine beasts. The result was a rehabilitation of the dragon as a symbol of medieval heroism and mystery rather than a mere superstition.

## 1.3 Literary Societies and Chivalric Pageants

Enthusiasts formed literary societies devoted to studying and reenacting medieval culture. Some staged chivalric tournaments—part ceremonial, part theatrical—where "dragon" effigies might appear for knights to defeat. Though playful, these events were serious attempts to reconnect with a storied heritage. Dragons, once nearly exiled from serious discourse by Enlightenment rationalists, now found a place in imaginative recreation of the "Age of Chivalry."

---

# 2. The Rise of Folklore Studies and Fairy Tales

## 2.1 Early Folklorists and Story Collectors

In the early 19th century, figures like the Brothers Grimm in German territories began collecting oral tales from rural communities, preserving them in written anthologies. The Grimms, along with other folklorists across Europe—Joseph Jacobs in England, Peter Christen Asbjørnsen and Jørgen Moe in Norway, and many others—discovered numerous references to dragons or dragon-like monsters in local legends, proverbs, and fairy tales.

## 2.2 Dragon Motifs in Collected Tales

Folklore anthologies revealed common dragon motifs: a fearsome reptile demanding tribute, a princess or village threatened, a brave hero (often a peasant lad) who outwits or slays the beast. In some stories, the dragon hoarded treasure underground or inhabited a mountain cave. In others, the dragon was multi-headed, echoing older Greek or Slavic influences. Folklorists classified these motifs, noting parallels across languages and regions.

## 2.3 Significance of the Dragon in Folk Narratives

While the Enlightenment had approached dragons as illusions, 19th-century folklorists took them seriously as symbolic elements within communal storytelling. They debated whether dragons represented primal fears (famine, storms), historical invaders, or moral evils. Romantic thinkers, for their part, cherished dragons as living remnants of an enchanted worldview. The "folk dragon" thus bridged rational scholarship and imaginative longing for an age of legend.

---

## 3. Local Legends, Festivals, and National Identity

### 3.1 Revival of Dragon Festivals
In certain towns, older pageants featuring dragons—sometimes dating back centuries—had faded or morphed over time. The 19th-century romantic wave encouraged revival. Civic leaders resurrected the local "dragon parade" or "dragon dance," proclaiming it a cherished custom that symbolized the town's ancient heritage. New songs, costumes, and decorations were devised, blending authentic tradition with romantic embellishment.

### 3.2 National Epics and the Dragon's Emblem
Nations in search of unifying symbols latched onto medieval or legendary dragons. Wales, for instance, reaffirmed the red dragon (Y Ddraig Goch) as a national emblem, linking it to Celtic pride. In parts of the German states, references to the dragon-slaying Siegfried became a rallying point for those seeking a cohesive German identity. In the Slavic world, serpent- or dragon-like creatures in local epics found renewed significance amid movements for cultural autonomy. Dragons, therefore, transitioned into heralds of national revival.

### 3.3 Eisteddfods, Feiseanna, and Similar Gatherings
Cultural festivals—like the Welsh Eisteddfod or Irish Feis—showcased poetry, music, and legends. Often, dragon motifs surfaced in the recitation of old tales, in decorative banners, or in dramatic retellings. These gatherings combined scholarship (antiquarian interest) with popular celebration, forging a sense of shared lineage. Where the Enlightenment might have scorned the "superstitious dragon," romantic nationalism embraced it as an ancestral jewel.

---

## 4. Paleontology's Early Steps and Dragon Speculations

### 4.1 Fossil Discoveries and Media Sensation
Throughout the 19th century, fossil-hunters and geologists uncovered the remains of enormous prehistoric reptiles—ichthyosaurs, plesiosaurs, pterosaurs, and eventually dinosaurs like Megalosaurus or Iguanodon. The public was enthralled. Newspapers sensationalized these finds, describing them as "antediluvian monsters." Some readers and even a few scientists wondered if these fossils were linked to the age-old dragon myths.

### 4.2 Dragon Myths as "Fossil Memory"?
A handful of intellectuals proposed that old dragon stories might stem from distant ancestors stumbling upon giant bones and concluding that monstrous reptiles once lived among them. While not mainstream science, this idea circulated in popular articles. Romantic imagination leapt at the notion that folklore preserved a hazy recollection of real prehistoric creatures. Thus, dragons gained a new dimension: maybe they were not illusions but echoes of Earth's deep past, bridging geology and mythology.

### 4.3 Debates Within Scientific Circles
Serious paleontologists typically avoided calling dinosaurs "dragons," wanting precise terminology. Yet they recognized the public's fascination with the label. Museums capitalized on it to draw crowds: an early dinosaur skeleton mount might be nicknamed "the dragon of old." Meanwhile, antiquarian scholars corresponded with paleontologists about whether a certain local "dragon legend" corresponded to a region with notable fossil discoveries. While conclusive proof remained elusive, the dialogue revealed how the dragon's mythical presence found a curious synergy with emerging paleontology.

---

## 5. Fairy Tale Publications and the Dragon Archetype

### 5.1 Mass-Printed Fairy Tales
Technological advances in printing meant cheap, widely available books. Fairy tales and folk stories featuring dragons proliferated, catering to middle-class families who wanted moral or entertaining literature for children. Publishers often added lavish illustrations, showing a plucky child or cunning hero besting a dragon. Over time, these children's versions of dragon stories helped shape a

gentler, more whimsical image of the beast—though it was still dangerous, the emphasis lay on the hero's cleverness or bravery.

## 5.2 The Role of Illustrators
Illustrators like Gustave Doré and others produced iconic depictions of dragons for popular editions of fairy tales or epic poems. Their art blended romantic style—dramatic landscapes, detailed textures—with imaginative monstrous features. These visual representations circulated widely, reinforcing a collective notion of what "a dragon should look like." Though the specifics varied—some had multiple heads, others had wings—this 19th-century pictorial tradition significantly influenced modern fantasy imagery.

## 5.3 Evolving Morality in Children's Stories
In older myths, dragons symbolized evil or chaos. 19th-century children's tales sometimes softened that stance, presenting comedic or instructive narratives. A dragon might be vain or gluttonous, ultimately reformed by a child's purity. Alternatively, it remained a fearsome villain, but the hero overcame it with virtuous cunning rather than brute force. These stories taught moral lessons about courage, humility, or kindness—using dragons as a safe stand-in for adversity.

---

# 6. Scholarly Theories: Comparative Mythology and the Dragon

## 6.1 Early Mythographers
Figures like Jacob Grimm, E.B. Tylor, and other proto-anthropologists or mythographers began systematically comparing myths across cultures. They noticed how serpent or dragon motifs recurred in Europe, Asia, Africa, and the Americas. Some hypothesized a primordial "serpent cult" or an Indo-European root myth behind dragon-slaying heroes. While these speculations were not always rigorous, they signaled a shift toward seeing dragons as a universal symbol in human imagination, rather than localized illusions.

## 6.2 Allegorical Explanations
Certain scholars claimed dragons were allegories for storms, floods, or cosmic disorder—pointing to how heroes often overcame them to bring renewal. Others stressed moral allegory: the dragon as greed, sin, or moral corruption. These interpretations resonated with 19th-century romantic thinkers who appreciated

symbolic nuance. Dragons thus found new life as a flexible emblem for intangible human struggles, from environmental threats to internal vices.

### 6.3 Linguistic Roots and Etymology
Linguists traced the word "dragon" to Greek *drakon* (serpent) and noted parallels in Sanskrit (relating to serpents), suggesting an ancient Indo-European link. They also examined local terms for monstrous serpents across continents. Such philological work fed into the era's fascination with deep cultural lineages, supporting the notion that dragon myths might share distant, prehistoric origins. Although the field remained young, it sparked further curiosity about dragons as a unifying mythic thread in global storytelling.

---

## 7. Local "Dragon" Legends in the Industrializing World

### 7.1 England's Industrial Landscapes and Rural Lore
While factories rose in the northern counties, rural villages in England still cherished legends of dragons: the Lambton Worm, the Dragon of Wantley, or St. George's conquests. Antiquarians documented these stories, sometimes lamenting that modern progress overshadowed them. At country fairs, reenactments persisted, bridging old folk traditions with the new industrial age. The dragon endured as a nostalgic figure, offering an imaginative escape from mechanized reality.

### 7.2 Continental Europe: Railroad Lines and Dragon Rocks
Across Germany, France, Italy, and beyond, railroads now crisscrossed the land. Tourists ventured to previously isolated mountainous or forested regions, discovering local "dragon stones" or legends about serpents once haunting a cave. Travel guides capitalized on these romantic sites, marketing them as picturesque vestiges of a mythic past. The presence of modern transportation ironically facilitated broader awareness and celebration of ancient dragon lore.

### 7.3 Eastern Europe and the Balkans
In Slavic nations and the Balkans, where national awakenings took shape, old epics featuring zmeys or dragons surfaced. Poets and intellectuals used these figures to champion independence or cultural pride. Folklore societies compiled local tales of dragons punishing oath-breakers or protecting hidden treasures.

Even as modernization spread, these dragon motifs reasserted cultural identity, forging continuity with a heroic, partly mythical lineage.

## 8. Cross-Atlantic Connections: Dragons in the New World

### 8.1 European Immigrants and Folklore Transfer
As waves of European immigrants settled in North and South America during the 19th century, they brought their dragon stories with them. In immigrant communities, festivals or storytelling sessions kept the old legends alive. Over time, these mingled with local indigenous serpent tales or new frontier narratives about monstrous beasts in the wilderness.

### 8.2 The American Frontier and "Dragon" Tales
In the United States, travelers to the western frontier occasionally labeled large lizards or unfamiliar phenomena as "dragons." A newspaper article from a small town might sensationalize a "dragon on the prairie," though it usually turned out to be an alligator in a river or a known reptile. Meanwhile, romantic writers in the U.S. wove dragon references into tall tales, bridging Old World lore with the new land's sense of boundless possibility.

### 8.3 South American Serpent Lore
In parts of Latin America, indigenous communities had long traditions of water serpents or cosmic reptiles. European settlers or scholars sometimes called these "dragons," creating a hybrid set of myths. The 19th-century push for cultural identity among newly independent South American states also included retellings of local serpent legends. Some intellectuals integrated them into a broader romantic narrative of national heritage, paralleling developments in Europe.

## 9. Visual Arts and the Dragon's 19th-Century Renaissance

### 9.1 Romantic Painting and Sculpture
Artists of the Romantic era, like Eugène Delacroix or Francisco Goya, occasionally tackled mythical subjects, including dragons. Although Goya's works often ventured into dark, surreal imagery, others depicted flamboyant scenes of

heroic struggle. Dragons, as the ultimate monstrous force, offered an outlet for emotional intensity and dramatic composition. Exhibitions in major cities attracted audiences eager for glimpses of the fantastic rendered in vivid color.

### 9.2 Academic Art and History Painting

A parallel stream in academic or "history painting" portrayed medieval or classical scenes with meticulous detail. The figure of St. George or Siegfried slaying a dragon provided a perfect opportunity to display academic painting's emphasis on anatomy, historical costume, and emotional expression. Patrons, whether royal courts or private collectors, admired these works as high culture, bridging biblical or heroic tradition with refined 19th-century artistry.

### 9.3 Illustrations for Literary Classics

New illustrated editions of medieval epics, mythological compendiums, and fairy tales abounded. Illustrators developed a distinctive 19th-century style for dragons, combining medieval references (such as scaly wings, serpentine tails) with romantic flair (elongated forms, swirling backgrounds, dramatic lighting). These pictures strongly influenced popular conceptions of dragons, forging a link between textual tradition and visual imagination that persists in modern fantasy art.

---

## 10. Public Pageants, Operas, and Theatrical Dragons

### 10.1 Opera Productions

Grand opera thrived in the 19th century, often with lavish sets and special effects. Composers and librettists drew on legendary tales for themes. A dragon might appear on stage as part of a hero's trial—managed by stage machinery that breathed smoke or fire, enthralling the audience. These productions fused romantic music with medieval or mythical storylines, ensuring the dragon's presence in elite cultural venues.

### 10.2 Folk Theater and Community Dramas

At the village or small-town level, seasonal festivals and community dramas still featured "dragon-slaying" scenes reminiscent of older traditions. Some craft guilds took pride in building ornate dragon puppets, paraded through the streets. These events combined moral messages—good triumphs over evil—with a celebratory display of local artistry. The children who watched them formed lasting impressions of the dragon as both fearful and festively enthralling.

### 10.3 National Celebrations
When newly formed or reforming nations marked significant anniversaries or holiday parades, they sometimes used dragons to invoke a sense of historical continuity or mythic grandeur. For instance, a city's float might show a legendary founder slaying a dragon, symbolizing the triumph of civic virtue. Through these symbolic pageants, dragons remained woven into the 19th-century public psyche, standing for heritage, spectacle, and moral allegory.

---

## 11. Continuing Folklore Research: The Dragon as Archetype

### 11.1 Comparative Mythology Flourishes
By mid-century, scholars like Max Müller propelled comparative mythology to new heights, examining how solar or elemental allegories might underlie myths. In such theories, the dragon represented destructive storms or night devoured by the hero-sun. Although these theories have since been refined or questioned, they were influential in the 19th century, providing intellectual frameworks that took the dragon motif seriously as an ancient archetype.

### 11.2 The Grimm Brothers and Beyond
Jacob and Wilhelm Grimm, after pioneering fairy-tale collections, delved into broader Germanic philology. They noted how dragon-slaying threads linked to heroic poems like the *Nibelungenlied* and Icelandic sagas. Their academic successors extended this approach across Europe, collecting variations of the dragon-slayer motif. This scholarship bridged ethnology, linguistics, and literature, reinforcing the dragon's place as a subject of legitimate academic curiosity rather than mere superstition.

### 11.3 Emerging Ethnographic Societies
Ethnographic societies in Germany, France, Britain, and Scandinavia compiled journals featuring local and foreign myths. Submissions analyzed dragon legends from the Balkans, Celtic fringe areas, or distant colonies, seeking cross-cultural patterns. The 19th-century thirst for classification turned the "dragon" into a comparative category, fueling theories about monomythic hero cycles or

universal serpent symbolism. Though these theories varied in quality, they consolidated the dragon's standing as a rich folkloric phenomenon.

## 12. Class Tensions and the Dragon's Social Symbolism

### 12.1 Elites, the Bourgeoisie, and Peasant Culture
With industrial expansion, class divisions sharpened. Elites attended grand operas where dragons were stage illusions. The bourgeois middle class consumed widely distributed chapbooks of fairy tales. Rural peasants kept living traditions of local dragon folklore. Each group interacted with the dragon motif differently, yet the creature provided a shared reference point. A peasant's story of a local wyrm might amuse an urban reader, who recognized a parallel in the epic sagas they had read, bridging social divides.

### 12.2 Critiques and Satire
Some politically minded writers used the dragon ironically: to satirize oppressive aristocrats or unscrupulous capitalists as "dragons devouring the people's wealth." Newspapers or pamphlets might depict a factory owner as a smoky dragon looming over workers. This usage echoed earlier propaganda but adapted it to 19th-century social struggles. The dragon's negative connotation—tyranny, greed—remained powerful, providing a stark symbol for inequity.

### 12.3 Dragon Imagery in Worker Unions
A few worker-friendly societies or guilds ironically flipped the dragon symbol. For instance, a union might adopt a stylized dragon to represent its collective might, subverting the old association of dragons with oppression. These scattered examples highlight how the dragon, once a sign of monstrous force, could be co-opted by subaltern groups. Still, such uses were not widespread, overshadowed by more conventional symbols like the hammer or gear in emerging labor movements.

## 13. The Dragon in Children's Education and Moral Lessons

### 13.1 Sunday School and Moral Tales
As Sunday schools proliferated, teachers used simplified biblical references to

dragons—especially the dragon of Revelation or symbolic references to the devil—to illustrate moral lessons. Pupils learned that a dragon represented sin or spiritual adversity. Simultaneously, children encountered gentler dragon narratives in secular fairy tales, creating dual impressions: the dragon as an embodiment of moral evil, and the dragon as a magical creature in stories of wonder.

## 13.2 Literacy Campaigns and Chapbooks

Expanding literacy meant an explosion of cheap chapbooks and pamphlets. Some retold old dragon legends in simplified form for new readers. These texts encouraged moral virtues like bravery, honesty, and humility, with the dragon's defeat symbolizing the triumph of good. Others sold purely as thrilling escapism, featuring serial heroes who faced a new monstrous serpent in each installment—a precursor to later episodic fantasy forms.

## 13.3 Growth of Children's Periodicals

By the late 19th century, specialized children's magazines emerged, printing short stories, puzzles, and color illustrations. Dragons often starred in these tales. Some editorial columns discussed the difference between "real animals" and "fanciful creatures," teaching critical thinking while still indulging imaginative delight. Thus, the next generation of readers grew up with a balanced perspective: dragons were fictional, yet culturally significant and creatively inspiring.

# CHAPTER SEVENTEEN: DRAGONS IN EUROPEAN ROMANTIC MOVEMENTS

## Introduction

By the late 18th and early 19th centuries, Europe was awash in the intellectual and artistic currents of Romanticism. While the previous chapter examined how the 19th century restored dragons to a place of prominence in folklore and national narratives, this chapter focuses more intently on the Romantic Movement itself. Romantics rebelled against Enlightenment rationalism by championing emotion, nature, the sublime, and the mysterious. In poetry, prose, painting, and music, they sought grandeur and intensity of feeling, often turning to medieval and mythic sources for inspiration.

Dragons, with their fearsome majesty and deep mythical roots, became ideal symbols for Romantic artists and writers. They conjured the archaic wonder of medieval chivalry and the primal forces of nature. Romantics found in dragons not only echoes of the national epics and folktales that they cherished but also a powerful symbol of the wild, untamed spirit that they believed reason and industrial progress had stifled. In the sections that follow, we will explore how Romantic poets, painters, composers, and cultural movements embraced the dragon motif, transforming it into a vessel for awe, terror, and imaginative freedom. We will see how different European regions interpreted dragons differently under Romantic lenses, and how these portrayals influenced broader cultural dialogues about identity, nature, and the boundaries of human experience.

---

## 1. The Backdrop of Romanticism

### 1.1 Reaction Against Enlightenment Rationalism
The Enlightenment's emphasis on logic, empirical proof, and systematic knowledge had greatly diminished the literal belief in dragons. As we saw, by the turn of the 19th century, most scholars viewed dragons as folklore or allegory. Romanticism arose partly as a revolt against the Enlightenment's perceived sterility. Romantics found the everyday world too constrained by reason, craving

instead the supernatural, the passionate, and the heroic. Medieval myths, including dragon stories, offered potent glimpses of a lost age of wonder—an antidote to modern disenchantment.

### 1.2 Celebration of Medieval Heritage
Where Enlightenment thinkers had critiqued medieval religion and superstition, Romantics praised the Middle Ages as a wellspring of authentic culture, faith, and imaginative depth. Dragons, inseparable from knights, castles, and epic struggles, emerged as a perfect emblem of the medieval imagination. Rather than ridiculing them as illusions, Romantics depicted them as living symbols of an era's emotional truth—intimidating, majestic, and haunted by glimpses of the uncanny.

### 1.3 The Sublime and the Monstrous
Romantic philosophers and aestheticians wrote extensively about the "sublime," a concept describing experiences that inspire both terror and exaltation, such as towering mountains or tumultuous storms. Dragons, huge and dangerous, naturally fit within this aesthetic. A poet could evoke the monstrous silhouette of a dragon perched on a crag, stirring feelings that transcended ordinary fear—mingled dread, awe, and even spiritual ecstasy.

---

## 2. Dragons in Romantic Poetry and Literature

### 2.1 Revival of Medieval Epics
Throughout Europe, Romantic writers reintroduced medieval texts to the reading public in accessible formats. Germany had the *Nibelungenlied*, in which Siegfried slays the dragon Fafnir. Britain revisited Arthurian legends, sometimes hinting at dragons within peripheral stories. Translators and philologists published new editions, annotated with rapturous commentary about the raw power of these ancient tales. In so doing, they popularized the dragon-slaying episodes, emphasizing their emotional intensity over any didactic moral.

### 2.2 Original Romantic Poems Featuring Dragons
Some Romantics, eager to weave medieval imagery into new works, composed fresh poems starring dragons. These dragons might embody nature's fury or the hero's inner turmoil. For instance, a poet might set a lonely knight against a monstrous serpent, culminating not in a moral sermon but in a tragic or

bittersweet reflection on fate and mortality. Rather than representing mere evil, the dragon became an ambivalent force—both frightening and strangely sympathetic, a totem of nature's indifferent power or of lost mystical realms.

### 2.3 Symbolic Interpretations

In Romantic writing, dragons took on complex symbolism. Sometimes they appeared as guardians of hidden truths or hoarders of treasures that signified the poet's deeper yearnings—perhaps for artistic brilliance or spiritual enlightenment. Slaying or confronting the dragon might represent the artist's struggle with personal demons or the pursuit of the sublime. Though the moral binary of "holy knight vs. wicked dragon" persisted in some narratives, a more nuanced approach often prevailed, hinting that the dragon's defeat might also be the loss of a primal mystery.

### 2.4 Influence of Translated Eastern Texts

A handful of Romantic writers drew upon newly translated Asian works or travel accounts referencing dragons in China, Japan, or India. While these references were often filtered through Western exoticism, they broadened the dragon concept. Some Romantic poems portrayed dragons as wise, ancient beings associated with Eastern philosophies, thus challenging the older Christian dichotomy of "dragon as devil." This cross-cultural appropriation, though not always accurate, further expanded the dragon's range of literary possibilities within Romantic thought.

---

## 3. The Visual Arts: Romantic Paintings and Illustrations

### 3.1 Emphasis on Emotion and Nature

Romantic painters typically favored dramatic landscapes, intense lighting, and swirling atmospheres. When depicting dragons, they often set them in remote wilderness scenes—rugged cliffs, moonlit ruins, or storm-buffeted coastlines. These settings heightened the sense of danger and awe. The dragon's form, scaled and serpentine, fused with the tempestuous environment, visually manifesting the Romantic ideal of humanity's smallness before nature's grandeur.

### 3.2 Notable Romantic Artists and Dragon Imagery

While not every Romantic painter tackled dragons directly, some produced iconic works that included draconic forms. One might see a tableau of a hero, hair streaming in the wind, locked in single combat with a beast whose vast wings overshadow the sky. The sense of scale and atmosphere overshadowed precise anatomical detail—Romantics valued emotional impact above scientific accuracy. In some paintings, the dragon almost merged with swirling clouds or mountainous shapes, blurring boundaries between creature and environment.

### 3.3 Exotic and Medieval-Inspired Costume
Romantic art often indulged in "costume fantasy," mixing various historical or exotic elements for dramatic effect. A dragon in such paintings might have horns reminiscent of Eastern portrayals, combined with the body of a medieval European serpent. Knights might wear armor that was not strictly historically accurate but elaborately decorative. The result was an aesthetic fusion that placed the dragon in a timeless, dreamlike Middle Ages, reinforcing the genre's ethos of imaginative liberation from strict historical constraints.

### 3.4 Engravings and Book Illustrations
As printing technology improved, illustrated editions of Romantic poetry and reprints of medieval epics became common. Woodcuts and engravings depicted dragons with swirling lines and shadowy forms, accentuating the sense of menace and mystique. These visuals shaped popular conceptions, especially among literate middle-class readers who might not attend major art exhibitions. The synergy of text and image deepened the Romantic portrayal of dragons as intense, otherworldly forces that dwarfed human protagonists, both physically and spiritually.

---

## 4. Dragons in Music and Operatic Works

### 4.1 The Romantic Opera Tradition
Opera in the Romantic era embraced mythic and medieval themes. Composers sought spectacle and powerful emotional narratives. Dragons, as dramatic foes or symbolic presences, occasionally appeared in stage designs for operas set in legendary realms. Though singing roles for a dragon were impractical, the beast might manifest as a looming puppet or be evoked through orchestral motifs. In more abstract productions, the dragon could be suggested by lighting, shadow, or dancers, representing the monstrous side of the story's conflict.

### 4.2 Dragon-Slaying Scenes on Stage
A few lesser-known Romantic operas or musical dramas included explicit dragon-slaying episodes, building on medieval epics. The protagonist's heroic aria might climax as he marches offstage to confront the beast, followed by tumultuous orchestral passages symbolizing the battle. Stage contraptions might produce "dragon roars" or plumes of smoke, culminating in the hero's triumphant reentry. Though possibly awkward to stage, such scenes fulfilled the Romantic craving for spectacle and grand moral struggle.

### 4.3 Symphonic Poetic Interpretations
Some Romantic composers wrote symphonic poems inspired by literary sources. A composer might base an orchestral piece on the storyline of a local dragon legend—depicting, through musical themes, the dragon's approach, the terror of the people, the hero's confrontation, and the final resolution. Even if no singer portrayed the dragon, the swirling, dramatic music conjured images in the audience's imagination. Thus, the dragon became a muse for the sonic expression of primal dread and heroic fervor, aligning with Romantic ideals that music should plumb the depths of human emotion.

---

## 5. Regional Variations of Dragon Romanticism

### 5.1 German-Speaking Lands
Germany (along with Austria and other Germanic states) had a wealth of medieval material featuring dragons, such as the *Nibelungenlied*. Romantic figures like Johann Gottfried von Herder, the Brothers Grimm, and Friedrich de la Motte Fouqué found in these sagas a powerful resource for national cultural pride. Dragons in these texts—particularly Fafnir—were reinterpreted as embodiments of greed or cosmic fate. German Romantic art often depicted dragon-slaying as a tragic, larger-than-life confrontation, reflecting themes of destiny that permeated the era's writing.

### 5.2 Britain and the Arthurian Revival
In Britain, the Romantic Movement intertwined with the medieval revival championed by Sir Walter Scott, Alfred Tennyson, and others. While King Arthur's core legends did not center on dragons, references to dragons swirled around peripheral tales of knights and beasts. Romantic-era poems sometimes connected the Welsh red dragon to Celtic myth, fueling a sense of historical

continuity. Paintings showed Arthurian knights or St. George confronting monstrous serpents. Dragons thus served as a unifying motif in the British quest for a heroic, chivalric heritage.

### 5.3 France and Neo-Medieval Inspiration
In France, Romantic novelists and poets like Victor Hugo or Alexandre Dumas occasionally invoked medieval or legendary beasts in their works, though dragons were less central than in Germanic or British traditions. However, the broader neo-Gothic architectural movement and medieval revival included draconic gargoyles or sculptural details that advanced the Romantic aesthetic. French illustrators produced lush images for reprints of chivalric romances, with dragons signifying the archaic enchantment that Romantics craved.

### 5.4 Eastern Europe and Slavic Dragons
In Slavic realms, including Russia and the Balkans, the Romantic rediscovery of folk epics brought to light local serpent or dragon-like figures—such as the Zmey, often portrayed in heroic songs. National awakenings harnessed these myths to celebrate an independent cultural spirit. Poets adapted or expanded these tales, weaving dragons into the struggle for autonomy from larger empires. Romantic imagery of dragons, either battered by a peasant hero or symbolizing ancient land-spirits, expressed both the grandeur of the old traditions and the yearning for modern self-determination.

---

## 6. Romantic Interpretations of Non-European Dragons

### 6.1 Exoticism and the Far East
As colonial ties expanded, Western Romantics also gazed upon Asia with fascination. While the previous century had introduced some knowledge of Chinese dragons as benevolent symbols, 19th-century Romantic exoticism magnified these creatures into emblems of an otherworldly realm. Artists might paint "Chinese dragons" with swirling clouds, referencing stylized Eastern art but imbuing it with their own sense of dreamy exotic longing. Writers penning Orientalist poems might describe desert caravans encountering serpentine beasts in remote oases, mixing inaccurate details but capturing a sense of imaginative escapism.

## 6.2 Blurring Boundaries Between Fact and Myth

The Romantic fetish for the unknown sometimes led authors to conflate real colonial findings about large reptiles with mythical dragons. Tales of giant Komodo monitors or other large lizards reached Europe, fueling speculation in diaries or short stories. Rather than treat them as mere zoological curiosities, Romantics might interpret them as living fragments of an ancient mythic order—"the last dragons," perhaps, lurking in shadowy corners of the earth. This approach satisfied the Romantic hunger for wonder and a sense of the world's hidden marvels.

## 6.3 The Middle East and Biblical Allusions

Travelers to the Holy Land or surrounding regions encountered desert ruins and local legends of monstrous serpents. In Romantic writing, these sometimes morphed into biblical-flavored narratives featuring dragons as symbols of demonic forces still haunting the cradle of faith. Illustrations for travelogues or Orientalist paintings might show a lone pilgrim overshadowed by a serpentine beast, dramatizing the confluence of scriptural resonance and the Romantic quest for dramatic, spiritual landscapes.

---

# 7. Philosophical and Psychological Readings of Dragons

## 7.1 Romantic Exploration of the Subconscious

While formal psychoanalysis belonged to a later era, some Romantic poets and thinkers explored the "dark side" of the human mind—repressed desires, nightmares, and spiritual crises. Dragons often figured as external manifestations of inner turmoil. In a narrative or poem, confronting the dragon signified grappling with unbridled passions or forbidden urges. This interpretation expanded the dragon's meaning beyond a purely external threat, hinting that the real "monster" might dwell within.

## 7.2 The Dragon's Duality: Evil vs. Insight

Romantics sometimes portrayed dragons not only as savage but also as strangely wise, echoing older Eastern lore. The beast might utter cryptic truths to the hero who dares approach. In such depictions, the dragon became a threshold guardian—frightening yet offering higher knowledge. This duality mirrored Romantic ambivalence about nature itself: simultaneously destructive and revelatory, terrifying and uplifting.

### 7.3 Political and Social Allegories
Some radical or liberal Romantics in Europe used dragon symbolism as a critique of oppressive regimes. A tyrannical monarchy or entrenched aristocracy might be labeled a "dragon devouring the people." Conversely, conservative Romantics might see revolutionaries as "chaotic dragons" threatening the social order. The shared language of draconic menace made it a convenient metaphor for swirling ideological struggles, fueling poems, pamphlets, or satirical engravings.

---

## 8. The Waning of the Romantic Era and the Dragon's Legacy

### 8.1 Shifts Toward Realism and Rationalism
By the mid-19th century, Realism rose in literature and art, challenging the Romantic obsession with fantasy and medieval nostalgia. Writers began focusing on contemporary social issues rather than legendary beasts. Meanwhile, scientific progress—especially the rising authority of geology, biology, and archaeology—pushed mythic creatures further into the realm of fiction. Yet the Romantic fascination with dragons never vanished; it merely lost its cultural dominance as a new generation favored more concrete portrayals of society.

### 8.2 Dragons in Late Romantic and Pre-Raphaelite Movements
Even as mainstream Romanticism ebbed, smaller groups continued to champion medieval aesthetic ideals. The Pre-Raphaelite Brotherhood in Britain, for instance, carried on painting richly detailed medieval and legendary scenes. Dragons appeared in their illuminations or decorative arts, stylized with elaborate, almost jewel-like craftsmanship. This offshoot of Romanticism kept the medieval dream alive, bridging the gap to subsequent fantasy-oriented currents that would flourish later.

### 8.3 The Dragon's Shift from Sublime to Beloved
Where early Romantics had portrayed dragons as embodiments of dread and cosmic power, late 19th-century reworkings often softened them into more whimsical or moral fairy-tale roles—especially in children's literature. This shift set the stage for the broad 20th-century spectrum of dragon portrayals, ranging from terrifying monsters to friendly companions. By the 1860s and 1870s, some moral or comedic plays featured a "dragon" cameo that audiences found endearing rather than petrifying, reflecting an evolving public perception.

## 9. Assessment of the Romantic Dragon Phenomenon

### 9.1 Key Contributions of Romanticism
Romantics rescued dragons from the purely allegorical or dismissive Enlightenment viewpoint, allowing them to reenter cultural discourse as living symbols of an imagined medieval past. They emphasized the emotional resonance of dragons: their capacity to evoke terror, longing, or awe. They also expanded the dragon's interpretive range—no longer just a monstrous devil, the dragon could represent nature's grandeur, the hero's unconscious, or the intangible forces shaping human destiny.

### 9.2 Tensions Within the Movement
Not all Romantics embraced dragons equally. Some found them too closely tied to superstition, preferring other medieval or mythic figures. Others criticized the insertion of dragons into pseudo-historical epics as frivolous escapism. Nevertheless, the majority recognized dragons as compelling icons of the unknown. In popular culture, the image of the rampaging or wise dragon enthralled audiences, fueling a steady demand for paintings, poems, and pageants steeped in medieval fantasy.

### 9.3 Influence on Later Cultural Developments
Though the Romantic era gradually yielded to other intellectual movements, its reimagining of dragons left a deep imprint. Later fantasy authors, from the late 19th century onward, drew heavily on Romantic concepts of heroic grandeur and dark sublimity. Folklorists continued referencing Romantic interpretations when analyzing local legends. Even budding scientists who wrestled with fossil remains sometimes invoked the Romantic notion of "ancient dragons." Thus, the Romantic dragon phenomenon forged a foundation for the modern fantasy tradition, bridging medieval heritage, emotional intensity, and imaginative possibility.

# CHAPTER EIGHTEEN: DRAGON RELICS, SIGHTINGS, AND STRANGE EVIDENCE

## Introduction

Throughout history, people have presented alleged "dragon relics" and reported "dragon sightings" that sparked wonder, debate, or outright fraud accusations. Medieval cathedrals once displayed bizarre bones as proof of a saint's victory over a monstrous serpent; travelers circulated tales of winged reptiles lurking in far-off forests; local legends boasted about precious scales or horns taken from a slain beast. Even into the 19th century, rumors of dragon remains occasionally resurfaced, fueling curiosity among the general public and skepticism among increasingly empirical-minded scholars.

In this chapter, we delve into the long tradition of purported dragon relics and sightings, examining how they shaped belief and fueled controversies. We will see how these claims often arose at cultural crossroads—cathedrals seeking relic-based prestige, merchant routes facilitating the trade of odd curios, or frontier regions where oral myth met travelers' thirst for sensational stories. We will also look at the roles of deception, misidentification, and genuine wonder in perpetuating the notion that tangible dragon evidence might be found in the real world. From ancient times through the late 19th century, these relics and sightings reveal a persistent human desire to anchor mythical dragons in material reality, even as scientific progress rendered the claim less and less tenable.

---

## 1. Ancient and Medieval Foundations

### 1.1 Early Apocryphal "Dragon Remains"
The practice of attributing large bones to dragons extends into antiquity. Greek and Roman authors sometimes mentioned colossal skeletons or giant teeth discovered in caves, which locals labeled as monstrous serpents or Titan remains. Later, in early medieval Europe, such finds were woven into Christian narratives, rebranded as proof that a local saint slew a demon in reptilian form. Although no systematic scientific method existed to verify these claims, the presentation of bones or horns in shrines cemented local legends, spurring pilgrimages and further embedding "dragon relics" into communal identity.

## 1.2 Medieval Reliquaries and Cathedral Displays

By the High Middle Ages, certain churches prized "dragon bones" as relics nearly as valuable as saintly remains. The public, entering a cathedral, might see a gigantic rib or skull suspended on a wall, labeled as the monstrous trophy from a legendary battle. Whether these items were mammoth bones, whale ribs, or dinosaur fossils was rarely questioned by believers. The narrative of a brave bishop or knight defeating a demonic beast gave the relic enormous devotional power, while boosting the site's prestige. This practice continued well into the Renaissance, though some Renaissance scholars quietly voiced doubts.

## 1.3 Impact on Local Legends

The presence of a displayed "dragon relic" could solidify and perpetuate local legends. Balladeers composed songs about the valiant hero who struck down the beast. Annalists chronicled the event in monastic records, embellishing details over time. As a result, the relic served as a tangible anchor for oral tradition, ensuring that the memory of a dragon-slaying act endured for centuries, even if the actual item in question might have originated from entirely natural—and non-draconic—sources.

---

# 2. The Trade in Oddities and "Dragon Parts"

## 2.1 Medieval to Early Modern Curiosity Markets

Well before the Age of Exploration, a modest market existed in "monstrous" artifacts. Merchants, apothecaries, and collectors of wonders circulated items like "dragon teeth," "dragon blood," or "dragon eggs," often mislabeled or fabricated. Genuine large reptile fangs from crocodiles or pythons might be sold as "dragon teeth," while red resin called "dragon's blood" came from the Dracaena plant. Buyers, whether seeking exotic medicines or collecting curiosities, fueled this commerce by paying high prices for anything rumored to be draconic.

## 2.2 Renaissance Cabinets of Curiosities

The Renaissance saw the rise of "cabinets of curiosities," where noble or scholarly collectors displayed rare natural specimens, artwork, and alleged monstrous remains. A "dragon skull" might occupy pride of place, surrounded by seashells, fossils, and stuffed birds from distant lands. While the cabinet owner might suspect a crocodile skull or fish bones, the item's label as "dragon" heightened its allure. Some owners relished the mystique, resisting strict identification to preserve an aura of wonder. Others truly believed they possessed proof of legendary beasts.

### 2.3 Apothecaries and Medicinal Uses
During the early modern era, "dragon parts" appeared in certain medical treatises. Powdered "dragon bone" might be recommended for ailments, or "dragon's blood" resin for wound treatment. Apothecaries across Europe and Asia occasionally conflated real substances derived from snakes, lizards, or mineral resins with mythical labels to boost sales. While more educated physicians increasingly dismissed such remedies, some rural communities and traditional healers clung to them, further disseminating the idea that actual dragon remains offered potent cures.

---

## 3. Age of Exploration: Renewed Claims and Discoveries

### 3.1 Colonial Curios and the "Dragon Trade"
With European voyages to Africa, Asia, and the Americas, the supply of strange animal materials expanded. Explorers brought back crocodile hides, anaconda skins, and other reptilian curios. Merchants and collectors at home sometimes advertised them as dragon relics, capitalizing on the public's appetite for marvels. Though scientists gradually identified these specimens as belonging to known species, many common folk remained convinced they were from actual dragons living in far-flung jungles or swamps.

### 3.2 Travelogues and Sightings Abroad
Colonial-era travelers occasionally published sensational accounts of "dragon sightings." A soldier in a remote African post might claim to have glimpsed a winged reptile at dusk, or a trader in Southeast Asia might retell local stories of giant serpents. Such stories, circulated in pamphlets, fed the belief that somewhere, beyond Europe's well-mapped lands, dragons thrived. While explorers often pointed to plausible animals like the Komodo dragon, these partial truths only fueled imaginative leaps.

### 3.3 Early Skepticism vs. Popular Enthusiasm
Learned societies in major capitals began receiving these alleged dragon relics for study. Naturalists dissected them, concluding they were hoaxes or mislabeled animals. Despite these debunkings, the mass public, enamored with tales of overseas wonders, remained receptive to the possibility. Newspaper headlines

still flared with rumored "dragon hunts," making official retractions less exciting to read. Thus, the Age of Exploration extended the phenomenon of uncertain sightings and questionable relics, even as a rational minority tried to quell the hype.

## 4. Post-Enlightenment Doubts and Romantic Curiosities

### 4.1 Enlightenment-Era Challenges to Dragon Artifacts
During the late Enlightenment, formal inquiries into cathedral relics or museum oddities uncovered numerous cases of mistaken identity. Commissions found that "dragon jaws" were whale mandibles, "dragon ribs" were mammoth bones, and so forth. While some church officials quietly put these relics in storage to avoid scandal, others continued displaying them, rebranding them as symbolic rather than literal.

### 4.2 The Romantic Revival of Relics
In the 19th century's Romantic wave, certain communities seized upon "dragon relics" to reinforce local legends. Rather than dismiss them as superstitious, they reframed them as "historical treasures from heroic times." Tourists enthralled by medieval nostalgia visited these relics, snapping up souvenirs or postcards (in places where printing was advanced enough). Even as skepticism grew in academic circles, the romantic imagination permitted a fresh appreciation for "authentic" relics, albeit often as cultural artifacts rather than proof of real monsters.

### 4.3 Literary Exploits
Romantic-era writers occasionally built entire novels or poems around a discovered dragon relic, conjuring a narrative of lost medieval battles or a saint's miraculous deed. Such fictional works blurred the line between reality and invention. Readers might come away uncertain whether the story was based on a genuine relic or a mere literary conceit, perpetuating a mild aura of belief in hidden draconic remains.

## 5. Scientific Examinations and Hoaxes

### 5.1 Early Paleontological Approaches
As the nascent science of paleontology emerged in the 18th and early 19th

centuries, scientists recognized that large fossils once attributed to dragons could be dinosaur remains or other prehistoric creatures. Scholars like Georges Cuvier in France demonstrated anatomically how many "dragon bones" matched extinct species that bore no direct relation to mythical winged serpents. Publications explained these findings, diminishing the credibility of church or castle "dragon relics."

### 5.2 Dissections of Alleged "Baby Dragons"
A recurring phenomenon saw traveling shows or curiosity peddlers displaying pickled or mummified "baby dragons." Natural philosophers who managed to inspect these specimens found them to be combinations of fish, lizard, or bird parts stitched together—a cunning taxidermy trick. Magazines of the time reported these hoaxes, sometimes ridiculing gullible audiences. Yet the cycle persisted: unscrupulous entertainers created new "dragons," and the public, enthralled by the possibility, kept paying to see them.

### 5.3 Motivations for Hoaxes
Some hoaxes were purely financial. Others had deeper roots: local patriots might craft a "dragon skull" to bolster a heroic legend, or a monastery might fabricate relics to attract pilgrims. Still others were pranks by amateur naturalists testing the credulity of the public. The varied motives underscore the cultural power of dragons—despite mounting evidence against their existence, the legend's allure inspired people to create illusions rather than let the myth fade away.

---

## 6. Rural "Dragon Sightings" and Communal Belief

### 6.1 Folkloric Continuity in the Countryside
Away from major cities and scientific institutions, local communities through the 18th and 19th centuries often retained belief in occasional "dragon sightings." A farmer might claim to see a large winged shadow pass overhead at dusk, or a shepherd might discover strange footprints near a cave. Villagers, already steeped in legends, interpreted any ambiguous sign as proof the local wyrm still roamed. Even if these tales never reached scholarly ears, they persisted in oral tradition.

### 6.2 Explanations and Rumors
Such sightings often had rational explanations: an unusually large eagle or flock of birds seen in poor light, a trick of shadows near a rock formation, or perhaps a

real creature like a giant bat in tropical regions. Yet rumor mills thrived on the sensational, embellishing each retelling until the "winged creature" grew to monstrous dimensions. In these close-knit villages, a collective sense of identity might hinge on the local dragon story, deterring naysayers from spoiling the fun.

### 6.3 Visiting Skeptics and Investigations
Sometimes, traveling antiquarians or minor government officials took an interest. They might camp near the rumored lair, find only normal animals, and declare the story false. Locals might then spin a new variation—claiming the dragon could turn invisible or had moved to another ridge. The clash between external skepticism and local myth left each side unconvinced by the other, reflecting a broader tension between rural folklore and the era's rational ethos.

---

## 7. The Role of Local Holy Figures and Saints

### 7.1 Continuing Veneration of "Dragon-Slaying" Saints
Despite Enlightenment critique, church calendars and local festivals still honored saints credited with dragon-slaying. Parishes told how St. Martha defeated the Tarasque in France, or how St. George saved a town from a devouring serpent. Relics—bones or tattered scales—remained on display as part of the saint's miracle legacy. Occasional sightings of a "ghost dragon" were said to confirm the saint's watchful protection, though church authorities often walked a fine line between promoting devotion and avoiding overt superstition.

### 7.2 Pilgrimages and Rituals
Certain shrines specialized in "miraculous cures" linked to the saint who overcame a dragon. Pilgrims might pray before the alleged fang or scale, seeking deliverance from personal evils. Over time, these devotions combined Christian theology with older local serpent worship patterns. The faithful might treat the relic as a channel of divine power, ironically giving new vitality to beliefs in dragons that official theology otherwise deemed purely symbolic.

### 7.3 Transitioning Toward Symbolism
Over the 19th century, many ecclesiastical authorities began more openly admitting the "dragon" was symbolic, while still affirming the saint's spiritual victory. By reframing relics as historical curios or tokens of faith, they preserved the shrine's significance without insisting on literal authenticity. Nonetheless, some devout communities clung to a literal reading, ensuring pockets of living belief that the relic indeed came from a real dragon once terrorizing the land.

# 8. Frontier Myths and Legendary "Dragon Lairs"

## 8.1 Remote Regions of Europe

In mountainous or forested areas—the Alps, the Carpathians, the Pyrenees, the Scottish Highlands—19th-century locals often pointed to caves known as "dragon lairs." Hikers or prospectors occasionally vanished or came back with tales of strange growls echoing in darkness. Natural phenomena like underground rivers or odd rock formations might produce eerie sounds, fueling speculation. Some adventurous travelers stoked these myths, writing travelogues that amplified the sense of forbidding mystery.

## 8.2 Colonial Frontier "Dragons"

Outside Europe, in colonial territories, certain deep jungles or deserts gained reputations as dragon-haunted. Explorers or missionaries might claim they heard roars at night or glimpsed "scaled horrors." In reality, these could be large cats, crocodiles, or unfamiliar reptiles. Yet each generation's retellings layered the story with more detail. With limited scientific oversight in such remote areas, sightings gained momentum, eventually traveling back to Europe as "proof" that dragons persisted in savage lands.

## 8.3 Folklore as a Defensive Tactic

In some frontier communities, rumor of a fierce "dragon" might deter outsiders from entering sacred or resource-rich zones. Indigenous peoples who used revered serpent spirits in their spiritual practice recognized how colonists or travelers spooked easily at tales of monstrous reptiles. The label "dragon" was easily understood by outsiders, so weaving it into warnings helped protect certain communal grounds or holy sites from intrusion—a subtle form of cultural and ecological defense.

---

# 9. Strange Natural Phenomena and Draconic Explanations

## 9.1 Meteorites, Celestial Lights, and "Flying Dragons"

Throughout recorded history, but continuing well into the 19th century in rural areas, sudden lights in the sky—meteors, auroras, or atmospheric oddities—might be interpreted as dragons in flight. Thunder and lightning storms, especially in mountainous regions, reinforced the idea of a roaring, fire-breathing reptile overhead. Folklore spread among peasants that a dragon soared among the clouds, spitting fire. The slow infiltration of scientific explanations for meteorology and astronomy did not wholly displace these beliefs, which held fast in local traditions.

### 9.2 Volcanic Activity
In volcanic regions like southern Italy, the idea of dragons inhabiting fiery underworlds had old roots. Occasional quakes or eruptions that roared beneath the earth might be described as the "dragon awakening." Romantics who visited these sites wrote poetic accounts linking volcanic fury to a draconic presence. Even though geology advanced knowledge of tectonics, imaginative visitors maintained that the "earth dragon" stirring the magma symbolized nature's unstoppable might.

### 9.3 Fossil Fuels and "Dragon Breath"
In coal-mining districts, pockets of gas could ignite, creating eerie flames in abandoned shafts. Local miners sometimes called these flares "dragon breath," consistent with older legends of serpents dwelling underground. Accidental methane explosions heightened the association. The 19th century's industrial expansion ironically introduced new forms of "fiery phenomena" that, in certain local contexts, merged with older dragon lore to explain bursts of flame or noxious vapors beneath the earth.

## 10. Literary Exploitation of Dragon Relics and Sightings

### 10.1 Gothic Novels and Dark Romances
The Gothic literary mode, overlapping with Romanticism, embraced haunted castles, cryptic manuscripts, and monstrous revelations. Some Gothic novels included subplots about an ancient dragon lair, complete with suspicious "bones" or rumored sightings. Authors used these elements to heighten dread and mystery, even if the dragon never physically appeared. The idea that a looming draconic presence overshadowed the castle or moorland lent the narrative a potent, chilling atmosphere.

### 10.2 Pulp Serials and Adventure Tales
By the mid- to late 19th century, cheap serialized magazines or "penny dreadfuls" offered sensational stories to a broad readership. A storyline might revolve around a relic stolen from a cathedral, believed to be the fang of a cursed

dragon, leading to supernatural curses or heroic quests. Though these plots were fictional, they recycled real historical legends about relics, weaving them into melodramatic escapism for an eager audience. This merging of authentic local lore with pulp sensationalism sustained the cultural presence of "dragon evidence."

### 10.3 Stage Plays and Melodramas
In popular theaters, managers produced melodramas featuring gallant knights, captive maidens, and the unveiling of "dragon bones." A comedic twist might reveal the bones were from a farm animal, fueling a moral about gullibility. Or a tragic twist might assert the relic truly belonged to a fearsome beast, foreshadowing its resurgence. The interplay of comedic skepticism and dramatic terror mirrored the broader cultural ambivalence—simultaneously mocking and craving the enchantment of dragons.

---

## 11. Learned Publications and Final Rejections

### 11.1 Academic Catalogs of Strange Finds
By the second half of the 19th century, major museums in London, Paris, Berlin, and other capitals published systematic catalogs of their collections, identifying mislabeled "dragon remains" with modern zoological or paleontological terms. A whale rib from a medieval cathedral, once claimed as a dragon bone, became "cetacean rib from the North Atlantic, 14th-century Europe." These publications, widely distributed among scholars, eroded the last vestiges of serious acceptance that any real dragon skeleton might be displayed in official institutions.

### 11.2 Paleontological Conferences
As paleontology advanced, experts met at conferences to discuss dinosaur genera, extinct reptiles, and other prehistoric life. They often ridiculed old claims of living dragons or monstrous relics, seeing them as remnants of a pre-scientific era. Indeed, the comedic contrast between rigorous fossil classification and folk claims of "fire-breathing serpents" underscored the shifting worldview. Where once "dragon bone" might earn local prestige, it now served as a cautionary tale about the power of myth over uncritical minds.

### 11.3 The Emergence of Skeptical Societies

Late in the 19th century, societies devoted to rational critique—proto-skeptical groups—began evaluating extraordinary claims. Dragon relics or sightings were prime targets. Published bulletins systematically refuted each new rumor, citing morphological evidence or referencing official museum reclassifications. The net effect was a near-consensus among academics that dragons were mythic, not biological. While pockets of lay believers persisted, the mainstream scientific community effectively closed the door on real dragons.

## 12. Cultural Impact and Legacy of Dragon Relics

### 12.1 Preservation as Folklore Heritage

As literal belief waned, some relics and alleged dragon bones remained on display in local museums or church corners, reinterpreted as part of cultural heritage. Labels might read: "Formerly Claimed as the Bone of the White Dragon Slain by Lord X—Actually Whale Rib from Northern Seas, 13th Century." This honest approach allowed communities to keep their legends alive as historical curiosity. Tourists appreciated the blend of myth and fact, while local guides told both the romantic story and the modern explanation.

### 12.2 Impact on Literature, Art, and New Media

The legacy of relics and sightings trickled into creative fields. Writers of historical novels set in medieval times referenced the old cathedrals with "dragon bones," or travelers in exotic lands chasing rumored beasts. Painters commemorated scenes of medieval parades presenting trophies of a dragon's head. Even after the mythic dimension was academically dispelled, it thrived as imaginative fuel, shaping the continuing fascination with dragons in all forms of storytelling.

### 12.3 Foreshadowing Modern Fantasy

Though we are avoiding modern references, we can note that the 19th-century romantic embrace of dragon legends, combined with the debunking efforts around relics and sightings, laid groundwork for the dragon to transition fully into the realm of fantasy literature and symbolic myth. The notion that actual physical dragons might roam the earth receded, but the cultural significance of "dragon evidence" lived on as part of a deep, enchanting tapestry of folklore—ready to be rediscovered, reimagined, or playfully reactivated by future creators.

# CHAPTER NINETEEN: GROWING SKEPTICISM AND CHANGING VIEWS

## Introduction

By the mid- to late 19th century, beliefs about dragons reached a decisive turning point across Europe and, to some extent, in other regions influenced by European thought. Longstanding lore continued in rural communities, romantic portrayals of dragons flourished in literature and the arts, and some local shrines still displayed alleged relics. Yet, a new tide of skepticism—and fresh ways of understanding the world—steadily eroded the notion that dragons might be literal, living creatures.

In this chapter, we will look at how growing scientific inquiry, rising secularism, and an increasingly urban, literate society shaped changing views on dragons. We will see how new academic fields—from geology and paleontology to comparative religion—challenged or reframed the significance of dragon myths. We will also explore how shifting social and cultural attitudes prompted people to reinterpret dragons as folklore and cultural symbols rather than actual threats or devils. By the end of this period, although dragons survived in the public imagination, they did so in a more metaphorical or nostalgic capacity, marking the transition from living myth to treasured legend.

---

## 1. The Decline of Literal Belief in Dragons

### 1.1 Scholarly Consensus Against Living Dragons
As the 19th century advanced, virtually all natural philosophers and academics reached the conclusion that dragons did not exist as biological species. Earlier centuries had left open the possibility that unknown regions—dark forests, remote mountains, or unexplored colonies—might harbor them. But now, systematic exploration, the expansion of zoological knowledge, and the thorough debunking of "dragon relics" severely undermined such hopes. Scientific publications stated plainly that no credible physical evidence of dragons had emerged from any region on earth.

## 1.2 Popular Understanding Catches Up
Although academic circles arrived at a consensus relatively quickly, it took longer for popular views to adjust. For much of the earlier 19th century, newspapers still carried sensational dragon stories, and curiosity shows trotted out hoaxes. Yet, as mass education spread and the general public encountered scientific explanations in newspapers, pamphlets, and school lessons, the notion of a hidden dragon population quietly retreated into the realm of fantasy. By the final decades of the century, only the most remote communities or deeply traditional circles clung to the possibility of living dragons in literal form.

## 1.3 The Role of Secularization
Secularization also played a part. While earlier Christian teachings had sometimes interpreted dragons as diabolical forces or biblical symbols, a more secular age found fewer reasons to treat dragons as literal devils prowling the earth. Churches themselves often reclassified the old "dragon battles" of saints as allegorical or moralistic tales. This shift dovetailed with the broad cultural move from medieval religious cosmology toward a rational and scientific worldview, leaving little room for actual serpentine demons.

---

# 2. Growing Importance of Folklore and Ethnology

## 2.1 Folklore Becomes a Recognized Field
Around the mid-19th century, folklore studies blossomed into a more formal discipline. Scholars and collectors cataloged local legends, proverbs, and customs, seeing them as windows into cultural history. Dragons naturally formed a major element in these records. Instead of treating them as monstrous realities, folklorists analyzed them as symbolic narratives. They inquired why so many societies had serpent or dragon myths, how heroes overcame these beasts, and what moral or social lessons were embedded in these stories.

## 2.2 Ethnologists and the Comparative Approach
Ethnologists, a sister field to folklore, took a broader comparative stance. They examined dragon myths in Africa, Asia, the Americas, and Europe, seeking underlying commonalities. Some proposed that dragons stemmed from universal human fears (floods, storms, or large predators), while others argued for Indo-European mythic roots linking serpent-slaying episodes to cosmic battles. Although these theories varied in sophistication, they generally emphasized that

dragons were cultural constructs—symbolic or allegorical. The question of whether a living dragon roamed the earth no longer dominated the discussion.

### 2.3 Dragons as Cultural Artifacts

With skepticism firmly in place, many intellectuals began to see local dragon stories as cultural artifacts worth preserving. Far from scorn or mocking, they treated them with a kind of anthropological respect—these tales represented a people's creative interpretation of nature's dangers or moral conflicts. This approach contributed to a gentler, more appreciative attitude toward dragons, even as belief in their literal existence declined.

---

## 3. Changing Religious Interpretations

### 3.1 From Demon to Metaphor

In Christian contexts, the dragon had long served as a stand-in for Satan or evil. As theological scholarship advanced, many church leaders emphasized metaphorical readings of biblical passages involving dragons. Preachers might still mention the dragon from Revelation or the serpent in Eden, but they made it plain these were symbolic figures, not flesh-and-blood monsters. This stance lessened the impetus to see real dragons as diabolical agents in the present world.

### 3.2 Continued Veneration of Dragon-Slaying Saints

Nevertheless, devotions to saints like St. George, St. Margaret, or St. Michael persisted, complete with imagery of them defeating dragons. In rural parishes, festivals and processions re-enacted these mythic battles. The difference now was that church authorities typically explained the dragon as an emblem of vice or pagan idolatry conquered by Christian virtue. Pilgrims might still admire "dragon bones" at a shrine, but an increasing portion of the faithful understood these objects as relics of tradition rather than literal monster remains.

### 3.3 Interfaith Reflections

Interfaith dialogue also evolved. In mission lands, Christian interpreters no longer insisted so strongly that serpent-worship or serpent deities were actual dragons or devils. Instead, some recognized them as distinct religious symbols, akin to the Western dragon as a Christian allegory. While pockets of confrontation or misunderstandings continued, the broader climate of intercultural awareness and academic study of religion softened the old demonization narrative, favoring cultural respect (at least among more progressive or scholarly circles).

---

## 4. Rational Reinterpretations and New Symbolic Uses

### 4.1 Dragons as Metaphors for Social Ills
Social critics and political commentators in the late 19th century occasionally invoked the dragon as a metaphor for entrenched oppression or corruption. A journalist might say that a tyrant was "a dragon devouring the people," or that nepotism was "the dragon at the heart of our institutions." This usage reflected a shift: the dragon was no longer a literal threat but a figurative tool for highlighting moral or political struggles.

### 4.2 National and Regional Pride
In parallel, some communities reimagined their local dragons as positive or neutral symbols of regional identity. Where once a "dragon plague" threatened the land, the creature was now an emblem of the region's heroic past or distinctive folklore. Welsh pride in the red dragon, for example, grew into a broader assertion of cultural uniqueness. City emblems featuring dragons, once purely heraldic or defensive, became cherished markers of civic heritage, bridging tradition and modern pride.

### 4.3 Commercial and Artistic Appropriations
With the growth of urban economies, dragons began appearing in advertising, brand logos, or decorative motifs. A brewer might use a dragon in its signage to connote strength or tradition; an architectural firm might incorporate draconic gargoyles in neo-gothic designs. Thus, dragons gained new life in commercial contexts, often stripped of any literal or religious significance, and used simply for evocative or aesthetic impact. This practical adaptation underscored how dragons had become malleable symbols rather than fearsome beasts of living folklore.

---

## 5. Late 19th-Century Festivals and Public Reenactments

### 5.1 Evolution of Dragon Pageants
Local festivals that once highlighted the actual threat of a dragon (or commemorated a saint's victory) evolved into more theatrical or celebratory affairs. Instead of a solemn reenactment of an evil dragon's defeat, towns increasingly staged elaborate parades with colorful floats. The "dragon" puppet or mechanical figure might be comedic or whimsical, inspiring delight rather than terror. Often, the role of the knight or saint was played by a costumed official, child, or popular figure, turning the spectacle into a communal, lighthearted event.

### 5.2 Village and Town Tourism
As railways connected more places, tourism rose. Towns recognized that their "dragon festival" or local dragon legend could attract visitors seeking quaint traditions. Guides retold the old story of a savage beast menacing the countryside, yet assured guests it was now purely historical or imaginary. Inns and taverns adopted dragon-themed names, forging a tourism identity around the once-dreaded serpent. Such commercialization confirmed that the literal fear had faded, replaced by nostalgic or economic uses of the myth.

### 5.3 Influence of National Romanticism
National romantic movements across Europe also encouraged the revival of local legends, including dragon tales, as an expression of cultural authenticity. Organizers of folk festivals presented these stories with pride, layering them with dance, costume, and music. Attendees from cities or foreign lands applauded the spectacle, seeing it as a charming glimpse into a region's soul. Yet behind the scenes, folklorists guided these revivals with an academic lens, shaping the narrative to highlight cultural heritage rather than literal superstition.

---

## 6. Shifts in Art and Literature Near Century's End

### 6.1 The Waning of High Romanticism
By the late 19th century, the grand epoch of Romanticism was yielding to Realism and Naturalism in literature and art. Many authors now tackled gritty social realities, not legendary beasts or medieval fantasies. Consequently, dragons

receded from high literature's central stage. However, they did not vanish; instead, they found new refuge in popular or children's literature, local pageantry, and the creative fringe of the era—particularly in the proto-fantasy genres that lay the groundwork for future imaginative works.

### 6.2 Illustrations in Children's Books
Publishers recognized a thriving market in children's stories that repackaged old dragon-slaying legends in a gentle, moral form. Illustrations showed bright, colorful dragons that might be menacing but also strangely endearing. The hero, typically a virtuous child or kindly knight, overcame the beast through kindness, wit, or bravery. By century's end, these stories were increasingly seen as beneficial for teaching values—courage, honesty—while also enchanting young readers with fantastical settings.

### 6.3 Early Hints of Modern Fantasy
A few late 19th-century writers began experimenting with fictional realms or "fairylands" inhabited by dragons. These works remained on the margins, overshadowed by Realist or socially conscious novels. Yet their existence foreshadowed a genre shift that would blossom later, where dragons occupied entire imaginary worlds. At this historical juncture, however, such imaginative fiction was considered niche, more akin to children's tales or whimsical curiosities than serious literature.

---

## 7. Archaeology, Geology, and the Final Reshaping of Dragon Lore

### 7.1 Advancing Geological Paradigms
Geology in the late 19th century gained robust explanatory power for Earth's strata, fossils, and prehistoric epochs. Scholars like Charles Lyell had advanced uniformitarianism, and their successors built upon these insights to reconstruct Earth's deep past. Fossil discoveries of large reptiles (dinosaurs, pterosaurs) became common in well-studied fossil beds. Scientists correlated these ancient creatures with the possibility that ancient peoples—finding colossal bones—had invented dragon myths. This hypothesis grew more mainstream: dragons were likely imaginative extrapolations from prehistoric finds.

### 7.2 Archaeological Investigations of "Dragon Sites"
Some antiquarians turned archaeologists examined reputed dragon lairs or old

castle archives detailing "dragon battles." They found, in many cases, traces of earlier pagan shrines or mundane evidence of a local conflict with wolves or invading armies. The "dragon" might have been a metaphor in medieval texts for destructive forces. In more literal narratives—like a fortress claiming a resident dragon skeleton—archaeological surveys confirmed misidentified bones or pure legend. These revelations rarely shocked local communities by this point; most had already accepted a symbolic reading.

### 7.3 Fossil Exhibits and Public Education

Museums displayed dinosaur skeletons in impressive halls, occasionally drawing parallels to dragon tales for the public's interest. Curators might put up signs that read: "Could this be the origin of dragon myths?" or "An actual prehistoric beast behind the legendary serpent?" While the official stance was that real dragons never existed in the medieval sense, the idea that ancient bones sparked stories caught the imagination. Visitors left these exhibits with a new perspective: dragons were no longer devils or unknown monsters, but distant echoes of Earth's reptilian past.

---

## 8. Rural Persistence, Urban Indifference

### 8.1 Stubborn Remnants of Fear

Despite widespread skepticism, certain remote districts clung to older beliefs. An elderly villager might warn children not to wander near a certain cave because "the old dragon might awake." These admonitions provided a convenient moral or safety lesson. While few truly expected to see a dragon, the tradition carried on as a half-joking, half-serious cautionary tale. Local superstitions about monstrous serpents, though rare, demonstrated how deeply mythic motifs linger outside scientific mainstream.

### 8.2 Urban Audiences and the Emergence of Nostalgia

In contrast, towns and cities, brimming with industry and social modernization, approached dragons with nostalgia or amusement. Journalists occasionally recalled "silly old dragon stories" to illustrate how far society had progressed from the darkness of ignorance. Yet ironically, many urban dwellers sought escape in romantic productions—operas, stage plays—featuring medieval knights and dragons, indulging in a sentimental yearning for a lost age of myth.

### 8.3 The Academic Middle Ground

Academic societies, bridging rural traditions and urban rationalism, documented local legends while disclaiming any literal belief. They recognized the anthropological and historical value of these dragon tales, collecting them for posterity. Conferences on folklore or philology might feature a paper on "The Last Dragon Legend of County X," analyzing how a village ceremony had changed over centuries. Thus, while the notion of actual dragons had faded, the stories themselves were preserved through a delicate balance of respect and scholarly detachment.

---

## 9. Class Dimensions of Belief and Skepticism

### 9.1 Elites and the Educated Classes

By late century, elites and the educated middle class viewed dragons almost exclusively as cultural or literary artifacts. Gentlemen scholars, museum curators, and polite society in parlors regarded it as quaint to think of real dragons. They might discuss "the dragon of yore" in intellectual or poetic terms but never as a serious zoological question. For them, the rational approach had definitively settled the matter.

### 9.2 Working Class and Rural Folk

The working class in growing industrial towns was often less exposed to advanced education, but they had daily contact with newspapers, chapbooks, and traveling shows. While they might enjoy sensational claims about dragons, many were not gullible; they recognized the difference between sideshow hype and reality. Rural folk, partly isolated from scientific institutions, maintained older customs or stories, though with diminishing conviction that these creatures were real. As a result, dragons dwelt in a half-real, half-legend sphere.

### 9.3 Patronizing Attitudes

Some upper-class commentators patronized rural communities, mocking their "superstition" regarding dragons. However, a subset of romantically inclined intellectuals championed these local traditions as preserving valuable cultural memory. This paradoxical attitude—both condescending and reverent—highlighted class divisions in how dragons were perceived: the illusory beast exemplified the quaintness of peasant belief for some, yet it also symbolized a deeper spiritual link to the land for others.

# CHAPTER TWENTY: THE LASTING LEGACY OF DRAGONS IN HISTORY

## Introduction

Across the millennia—through ancient civilizations, medieval Christendom, global exploration, Enlightenment critique, and Romantic re-imagination—dragons have maintained a stubborn presence in human culture. By the close of the 19th century, literal belief in living dragons had all but vanished from scholarly discourse, and among the broader population, dragons were increasingly seen as mythic or symbolic. Still, the dragon's hold on the collective imagination remained powerful, its imagery persistent in folklore, the arts, local rituals, and national emblems.

In this final chapter, we take a wide-angle view of dragons' enduring legacy. We will summarize their major historical roles, from guardians of nature's secrets to embodiments of evil or greed, from heraldic emblems of noble might to romantic icons of the sublime. We will explore how dragons continue to serve as cultural signifiers, bridging eras and geographies, embedding moral lessons, and uniting communities around shared symbols. We will conclude with reflections on the dragon's universal appeal—why this mythical reptile, despite countless cultural transformations, continues to spark fascination. In doing so, we see that dragons, though demystified as physical beasts, stand as enduring reminders of the human capacity for wonder, creativity, and the longing for the extraordinary.

---

## 1. Summation of Dragons' Historical Trajectory

### 1.1 Ancient Serpentine Beginnings
From the earliest records in Mesopotamia, Egypt, and other ancient realms, serpents and serpent-like beings shaped cosmologies, often merging with the concept we later call "dragon." These primeval serpents guarded cosmic gates, commanded rain, or threatened gods. By the time writing took hold, monstrous serpents appeared in creation epics, heroic tales, and religious rituals. While not always called "dragons," they formed the foundation for later draconic evolution.

## 1.2 The Medieval Christian Dragon

Medieval Europe reshaped dragons into devils and cosmic foes. The Church championed saints who defeated serpentine monsters, illustrating the triumph of good over evil. Dragons loomed in bestiaries and local legends as destructive or cunning forces, fueling both fear and moral resolve. Meanwhile, outside Europe, in Asia, Africa, and the Americas, serpent myths took varied forms—benevolent guardians, bringers of storms, or cosmic protectors. As trade and travel expanded, these traditions cross-pollinated, gradually broadening the dragon concept.

## 1.3 Enlightenment Skepticism and Romantic Revival

The 17th and 18th centuries saw dragons demoted to folklore and relic illusions, their existence challenged by scientific investigation. Yet Romanticism rekindled interest, viewing dragons as emblems of medieval heroism or the sublime power of nature. This resurgence placed dragons firmly in the realm of cultural myth, fueling literary and artistic works. Over the 19th century, the tension between romantic wonder and rational skepticism resolved into an understanding that dragons were potent cultural symbols rather than real creatures.

---

# 2. The Dragon's Enduring Roles and Symbolism

## 2.1 Guardian of Thresholds and Treasures

In many myths, dragons guard gateways, sacred waters, or hidden riches. This motif resonates across times and lands: from Greek myths of Ladon protecting golden apples to East Asian dragons presiding over watery realms. The notion that a formidable reptile sits at the boundary of the unknown underscores humanity's perception of "wild nature" as both bountiful and perilous. Even in the final chapters of dragon lore, modern(izing) societies recall the trope of a heroic quest involving a dragon-guarded hoard, signifying the difficulties and rewards of exploring uncharted domains.

## 2.2 Emblem of Evil, Greed, or Sin

In the Christian Middle Ages, dragons epitomized diabolical menace. Saints' battles with dragons stood for moral or spiritual victory. Even outside strictly religious contexts, dragons often represented destructive appetite—hoarders of gold, devourers of virgins—manifesting the dark side of human impulses. While Enlightenment critique and romantic reinterpretation softened the monstrous aspect, it never vanished: children's tales and moral plays continued featuring the dragon as a cautionary figure, whether about greed, pride, or unbridled power.

### 2.3 Symbol of Power, Royalty, and Identity

Dragons also served as positive or ambivalent symbols, especially in heraldry, where they connoted martial prowess or royal legitimacy. Rulers adopted dragon motifs to convey fearlessness. Over centuries, such usage transformed from literal war standards to decorative crests, bridging aristocratic heritage with cultural identity. Some nations integrated dragons into their flags or seals, forging an emblem of unity or historical continuity. Thus, dragons remind us how mythic imagery can become woven into political and communal identity.

### 2.4 Master of Elements and Nature

In Asia, dragons took on beneficial roles as controllers of weather and water, bestowing rain for agriculture. Certain African serpent traditions, labeled "dragons" by outsiders, performed similar ecological functions. Romantic artists in Europe recast dragons as embodiments of natural fury—lightning, storms, volcanic eruptions. Even in tales that cast them as villains, dragons often represented unstoppable elemental force, forging a persistent link between the beast and nature's raw grandeur.

---

## 3. Cultural Memory and Oral Tradition

### 3.1 Storytelling Across Generations

Well before printing, dragons flourished in oral tales, passed down at hearths and communal gatherings. Grandparents warned children about a lurking wyrm or recounted an ancestor's victory over a monstrous serpent. This practice sustained dragon lore through centuries of political upheaval. Even after literacy and printing spread, local storytelling sessions remained vital, giving each generation a living link to ancestral myths. As literacy rose, these oral accounts merged with or fed into written compilations, preserving them in folklore archives.

### 3.2 Local Legends and Place Names

Many regions bear place names referencing dragons—like "Dragon's Hill" or "Wyrm's Hollow." Such toponyms anchor the myth in physical geography, perpetuating stories even when belief dwindled. Visitors might ask, "Why is it called Dragon's Hill?" and a local would retell the legend. In this manner, the memory of dragons endures in the landscape itself, sustaining a quiet but persistent sense of enchantment around certain hills, caves, or lakes.

### 3.3 Folklore Variation and Adaptation
Over time, dragon tales adapt to new social realities. In some places, the older moral or religious dimension faded, replaced by comedic twists or romantic subplots. Elsewhere, new political events or heroic figures attached themselves to old dragon legends. Such fluidity highlights how dragons remain robust vehicles for communal storytelling—able to bear the imprint of each era's values while preserving a timeless core of wonder.

---

## 4. Dragons in Architecture and Art Across Eras

### 4.1 Gargoyles, Statues, and Decorative Motifs
From medieval cathedrals to 19th-century neo-gothic structures, dragons appear carved in stone, perched on spires or rainspouts (as gargoyles), or rearing above doorways. These forms marry practicality—like directing water away from walls—with symbolic resonance, reminding passersby of protective or frightening forces. Over centuries, styles changed, but the dragon's shape proved surprisingly adaptable. Nineteenth-century architects, influenced by romantic revival, renewed the tradition of draconic ornamentation, bridging old Catholic iconography with a modern appetite for the picturesque.

### 4.2 Fine Art and Stained Glass
In churches and civic buildings, stained glass windows sometimes feature dragon battles—St. George's confrontation or the apocalypse dragon from Revelation. These luminous scenes transmit both spiritual lessons and an enduring aesthetic fascination. Artists in the Renaissance or Baroque periods had put their own flourishes on such motifs, but even into the 19th century, renewed interest in medieval design prompted fresh commissions. This continuity testifies to how deeply dragons stayed embedded in visual culture, transcending theological shifts.

### 4.3 Romantic-Era Paintings and Sculptures
As we saw in the Romantic context, large-scale canvases or dramatic sculptures

captured knights and dragons locked in fateful struggles or placed the dragon in swirling natural vistas. Some 19th-century patrons, whether local lords or civic councils, commissioned monumental works that retold local "dragon" legends in grand style—reinventing them as part of the region's heroic identity. By century's end, dragon imagery, while occasionally overshadowed by Realist tastes, still thrived wherever medieval or mythical themes found favor.

---

## 5. Heraldry, National Symbols, and Civic Identity

### 5.1 Noble Families and Orders
Dragon symbols remained in the coats of arms for certain noble lineages. Although the original martial connotations had softened, these arms still projected an aura of venerable power. A family might trace its mythical ancestry to a knight who slew or tamed a dragon, preserving the story as genealogical lore. Orders of knighthood, some established centuries earlier, continued to bear insignias depicting dragons, albeit often with historical or ceremonial significance rather than active military use.

### 5.2 Municipal and Regional Emblems
Cities or regions that boasted a legendary dragon-slaying tale integrated the beast into their civic coat of arms, seals, or flags. Over time, as historical references to real dragons faded, these symbols took on fresh meaning as markers of local pride. In parades or official ceremonies, a stylized dragon might appear, no longer denoting fear but rather unity and tradition. Such usage underscores how myths can evolve from cautionary tales to rallying points for civic identity.

### 5.3 National Movements
In some parts of Europe, the 19th-century nationalist fervor revived archaic images, including dragons, as expressions of cultural uniqueness. The Welsh red dragon stands as a prime example, but other regions used serpentine creatures to highlight ancient roots. Whenever a new political formation emerged—like small principalities uniting into a larger kingdom—there was occasional discussion about adopting or maintaining draconic elements, reflecting collective memory and a sense of heritage continuity.

# 6. Moral and Didactic Functions

### 6.1 Teaching Through Dragon Tales
Dragons never ceased serving as cautionary figures in moral narratives. Whether in Sunday school lessons or secular children's books, the dragon's defeat by a pure-hearted protagonist conveyed clear messages: good triumphs over evil, humility counters pride, courage can overcome dread. Teachers found dragons effective for capturing attention, embodying negative traits in a thrilling form. By personalizing vice or sin in a monstrous reptile, moral lessons came alive for impressionable minds.

### 6.2 Allegories in Literature and Theater
Late 19th-century authors sometimes used dragon episodes to comment on contemporary issues. For example, a satirical play might depict a politician as a cunning dragon hoarding taxpayer gold, or a comedic story might show modern society's inability to face "the dragon of complacency." Audiences recognized these allegories, appreciating how the old monster still served as a flexible vessel for discussing greed, oppression, or social inertia.

### 6.3 Symbolic Rites of Passage
In some local traditions, young men reenacted a "dragon challenge," a symbolic test of bravery. The ritual might involve facing a puppet beast or venturing to the rumored dragon's cave at night. While participants knew no real serpent awaited, the drama forged communal bonds and tested personal fortitude. Such rites connected the present to ancient heroic models, reaffirming that even in an era of industrial progress, the dragon's trial still imparted valuable moral or social lessons.

---

# 7. Dragons as Romantic Nostalgia and Fanciful Escape

### 7.1 Retreat from Industrial Realities
Amid factories, crowded cities, and social upheaval, many people yearned for an imaginative escape to a "simpler," more mystical age. Dragons, along with knights, castles, and enchanted forests, offered precisely that. Books, stage plays, and visual art that evoked draconic imagery tapped into a collective desire for wonder. Even if the audience no longer believed dragons literally prowled the

outskirts, they found comfort and inspiration in conjuring them as mythic illusions.

### 7.2 Literary Clubs and Societies
In certain urban circles, reading clubs or societies devoted to medieval or romantic literature held gatherings to share knightly romances, epic poems, or fairy tales about dragons. Attendees might debate thematic layers—was the dragon symbolic of the hero's psyche, or a metaphor for natural disasters? Such discussions reinforced the idea that dragons had graduated from real possibility to metaphorical or psychological significance, reflecting how intellectual pursuit of legend thrived even amidst modern skepticism.

### 7.3 Popular Entertainments
Public entertainments—circuses, puppet shows, traveling illusions—often featured "dragon cameos." A clown might battle a papier-mâché serpent in comedic pantomime, or a puppet show might retell a local saint's dragon victory in miniature. These amusements appealed broadly, from children to adults seeking lighthearted nostalgia. The dragon's depiction varied from monstrous to playful, but in all cases, it underscored the creature's shift into a safe domain of imagination, no longer stoking real fear.

---

## 8. Persistence in Non-European Cultures under Colonial Influence

### 8.1 Syncretic Adaptations
In Africa, Asia, and the Americas, where serpent or dragon-like myths long predated European contact, colonial and missionary influences often recast local deities as "dragons." Yet by the later 19th century, as indigenous leaders and local intellectuals navigated new social realities, some reclaimed or reinterpreted these serpent traditions, emphasizing their cultural importance over colonial demonization. The result was a tapestry of hybrid beliefs—Eastern dragons mingling with Western iconography, African water spirits re-labeled but still revered in local ceremonies.

### 8.2 Local Nationalism and Cultural Revival
Colonies moving toward self-determination sometimes revived serpent or dragon lore as part of a cultural renaissance. Much like European national movements, these societies recognized that such myths, once scorned by

colonizers, could unify people around shared heritage. The "dragon" thus served as a reclaimed symbol of indigenous identity, conferring dignity on ancient traditions that had been dismissed. Even if the label "dragon" was foreign, the underlying serpent imagery rose as a sign of cultural reawakening.

### 8.3 Continued Tension with Christian or Rationalist Views
Nevertheless, Christian missions and colonial administrators still expressed wariness about serpent worship or "dragon cults," seeing them as superstitions to be combated or modernized away. Anthropologists, however, approached these beliefs with a more measured interest, acknowledging their complexity. By century's end, the old vehement battles over "heathen dragons" had cooled, replaced by academic curiosity or paternalistic attempts at assimilation. The net result was that local serpent traditions endured, albeit transformed by interactions with Western rationalism and Christian theology.

---

## 9. The Timeless Fascination: Why Dragons Endure

### 9.1 Dual Nature: Fear and Awe
A key reason dragons remain so enthralling lies in their duality: they evoke primal fear yet also command respect or even veneration. This tension resonates with fundamental human experiences—grappling with the unknown, feeling small before nature, yearning for heroic triumph. Whether we see a dragon as a vile monster or a wise guardian, the emotional impact remains profound, bridging eras and belief systems.

### 9.2 Adaptability Across Cultures
Dragons adapt to countless cultural frameworks. They can be holy or demonic, malevolent or benevolent, earthly or cosmic. This malleability helps them migrate across geographical and historical boundaries. Societies incorporate the creature's image into local religions, folk traditions, or political symbolism, tailoring it to their moral or existential themes. As a result, dragons serve as a cross-cultural mythic language.

### 9.3 Symbolizing Personal and Collective Quests
Dragons also symbolize the obstacles one must face—personal demons, moral failings, societal dangers, or hidden potentials. Heroes confronting dragons in epics or fairytales reflect universal arcs of growth and redemption.

Communities, too, battle their "dragons" of famine, strife, or injustice, forging narratives of resilience. The dragon's defeat or taming often heralds renewal, making it an evergreen motif for storytellers to express transformation and triumph.

## Conclusion: Dragons as Enduring Historical Symbols

From the earliest serpent deities to the medieval devourers of villages, from Enlightenment skepticism to Romantic celebrations, and from local relics to globally recognized icons, dragons have traversed every epoch. By the late 19th century, the question of their literal existence had found a final resolution among educated classes: dragons were myth, not biological reality. Yet that consensus did not diminish the dragon's cultural might. Rather, it opened new horizons for the creature to evolve into a purely symbolic, imaginative, and artistic presence.

In temples and cathedrals, on city flags and family crests, in fairy tales and stage productions, the dragon stands as a testament to human creativity and longing for the extraordinary. Over centuries, it has conveyed moral lessons, defined civic identities, buttressed religious teachings, spurred tourism, and fueled romantic fantasies. It has been demon, guardian, hoarder of gold, symbol of nature's wrath, and gatekeeper to spiritual mysteries.

Ultimately, the dragon's lasting legacy in history reflects our unending fascination with what lies beyond the familiar—those powers or forces that challenge our courage, test our morality, and remind us that the world once seemed (and may still be) wider and deeper than our ordinary senses permit. In the grand tapestry of human myth, the dragon occupies a central pattern: timeless, protean, and awe-inspiring. Through the ages, as scientific horizons expand and cultural forms shift, the dragon endures—no longer lurking in the edges of uncharted maps, but roaring loudly in the shared imagination, where it continues to thrive as one of humankind's most enduring and captivating symbols.

www.ingramcontent.com/pod-product-compliance
Lightning Source LLC
LaVergne TN
LVHW012106070526
838202LV00056B/5641